SIGNPOSTS TO KERRY

SIGNPOSTS TO KERRY

Nóra Relihan

Published in Association with

MERCIER PRESS
5 French Church Street, Cork
16 Hume Street, Dublin 2

Trade enquiries to COLUMBA MERCIER DISTRIBUTION,
55a Spruce Avenue, Stillorgan Industrial Park, Blackrock,
Dublin

10 9 8 7 6 5 4 3 2 1

FOR MARTINA AND MICHÈLE
AND IN
MEMORY OF MICK

Printed in Ireland by Colour Books Ltd.

CONTENTS

FOREWORD

Kerry is a place apart. Its rich heritage, captivating scenery, abundant wildlife and engaging people will all charm and seduce you, leaving you with an insatiable desire to explore the infinite magical delights that linger, just below the surface, to reward the curious and inquisitive traveller and native alike. Every rock, hedgerow and grassland or meadow has a fascinating tale waiting to be revealed. Every townland and village has a revered and honoured hero, whose memory lives on in the hearts and minds of its people. You could spend a lifetime in Kerry, but only manage to unearth a fraction of the anecdotes, legends, yarns, and the odd fib, that the county has to offer. A brief chat with a friendly local will unveil a wealth of material that you will not find in any book or journal. You may even gain an insight into the Celtic temperament, which, according to the writer Canon Patrick Agustine Sheehan, 'leaps to the weight of a feather; and you have sullen depression, or irresponsible gaiety, murderous disloyalty or more than feudal fealty, in swift and sudden alterations'. Good luck!

There is more than a trace of that sentiment in the stories that follow in this book. Radio Kerry commissioned Nóra Relihan to travel the county, chat to the locals, survive the 'sudden alterations' and to bring her adventures to life in a series of three-minute radio features. Nóra was eminently qualified. Her Kerry childhood, her connections with the Kerry railway, her artistic talents and credentials, her unrivalled sense of Kerry all contribute to her unique insight into, as James Joyce wrote in *Ulysses*, 'The now, the here, through which all future plunges to the past'.

The stories in this book were all written for the spoken word, but have been adapted to some degree to suit the written word. I sincerely hope they stimulate you to seek out your own undiscovered gem of wisdom as you ramble around the Kingdom.

> *But indeed everything red is beautiful, everything new is bright, everything unreachable is lovely, everything familiar is better, everything absent is perfect, everything known is neglected, until all knowledge is known.*

– Anonymous (ninth century) 'The Sick-Bed of Cuchulainn'.

Enjoy!

Paul Sheehan
General Manager
Programme Controller
Radio Kerry. April 2001

PREFACE

On a clear day, more than a million years ago, a leader named Ith stood on top of an old Roman lighthouse in Galicia in Spain – and saw Ireland! By origin Egyptian, and having conquered Spain comprehensively, Ith had become restless again and, thinking he'd like a taste of Kerry, he and some of his followers set sail in three ships and steered a steady course until they landed in Iveragh!

This story has survived the centuries and was no doubt handed down to us by the poets who, tradition-ally, were responsible for recording our *dinnsheanchas* – the folklore of our places – or topography.

Much adventure befell Ith and his followers. This collection offers you many vicarious adventures of your own in County Kerry. Indeed, it may encourage you to follow some of your chosen signposts, leading to a fort, a castle, a festival or maybe a memory, or wherever your fancy takes you in our Kingdom.

By the way, it was during the Fenian Cycle that Kerry became a Kingdom when the great Queen Maeve's son, Cian of Connaght, travelled south and called the whole county after himself – Ciarraige! And if legends hold a grain of truth in them, and you'd never know they might, you could hear some really tall tales while sitting on a jaunting car in Killarney and listening to the jarvey as you drive round Beauty's Home!

INTRODUCTION

For me, Kerry is 'Then and Now'. It is a magic lake – Caragh Lake, and a small girl sitting in a boat and warned to keep still while two older brothers dived into crystal clear water to retrieve pieces of soap. It is Cappanalea now with sophisticated adventure sports – and there is always Glencar to explore by bike or car.

Kerry is a memory of growing up in the Station House in Killorglin at the foot of the McGillicuddy Reeks and arguing about which peak in the range really is Carrantuohil, Ireland's highest mountain. It is also a saddle-sore memory of cycling seemingly endless miles through passes in the Reeks with names like Bealach Beama and Bealach Oisin; of watching mussels from Cromane on their way to France and wondering why we never ate them, but the signal-box man did – raw – after a few pints in the Railway Bar.

King Puck sat on his high throne for three days every August. Being used to him, a child's chief fascination was with the stalls, filled with treasure, that bordered the square, and of women in vast white aprons holding out a box of envelopes while encouraging passers-by to draw one, each using the same inviting catch phrase: 'A penny a draw and a prize each and every time – all prizes, no blanks'. Always a prize – wonderful!

Now, King Puck still sits on his throne and accepts

international homage. We all enjoy eating mussels and you can drive in comfort through the passes in the Reeks and enjoy the spectacular colour, changing with the seasons.

Then there was lovely Glenbeigh and the strand at Rossbeigh, with a wave to Inch across the way on the great Corca Dhuibhne Peninsula. We would take the train from Killorglin to Glenbeigh and walk from there the couple of miles to Rossbeigh Strand. At the end of each sunny, sandy day – exhaustion. And further on into the Iveragh Peninsula there is Carhan Bridge, a landmark of renown, and Sigerson Clifford country. As you approach his home town of Cahersiveen you might hear echoes of this well-known poet/playwright's best-known song, 'The Boys of Barr na Sraide'.

And Kerry for me can be a walk through Sandes Bog near Listowel, listening to the bird-song while marvelling at the colour. It is any bog road in what truly is – A Kingdom!

THE FERRY ROAD

A rare blending of several centuries is incorporated into the short winding road which links Tarbert Island and the Ferry Port with the village of Tarbert, where connecting roads lead to Limerick, Listowel and further along North Kerry's lovely coastline. Having disembarked from a state-of-the-art Shannon Ferry after a twenty minute crossing from Clare, and leaving the Electricity Board's huge generating station behind on the island, old black iron gates and a notice saying Tarbert House, Heritage House, beckons one to a unique seventeenth century, three storey house. Home to the Leslie family for three centuries, Tarbert House exhibits a mix of Queen Anne and Georgian styles.

The benign image of the Leslies as local landlords is supported by a plaque on an armchair in the Great Hall carrying the inscription 'Chair given to Robert Leslie of Tarbert House in 1846 on attaining his majority by the tenantry'. With a traceable ancestry stretching back to the Hungarian L'Esseles in the eleventh century, through the Scottish Leslies in the fifteenth century, the family finally settled in Tarbert in the seventeenth century. John Leslie, who died in August 2000, was the last head of the Leslie family to carry the title Seignior of Tarbert.

Built in 1690, Tarbert House retains its original form except for the inclusion of a second, wider staircase to accommodate the advent of the crinoline dress. Additional free-standing pieces illustrate the travels, interests and careers of the Leslie family through the centuries.

Famous visitors include Daniel O'Connell, Charlotte Brontë on honeymoon, Winston Churchill on school holidays, Benjamin Franklin on a trade mission, Lord Kitchener on a seaweed-gathering expedition for his arthritic mother's bath and Dean Jonathan Swift who wrote – typically – 'The Leslies have lots of books upon their shelves – all written by Leslies about themselves'!

Today's visitor may view by appointment.

Exiting from the Ferry Road to Tarbert village gives cause for a double-take as a life-size nineteenth-century constable comes into view. Standing outside the beautifully restored Bridewell, 'he' is actually welcoming the visitor to come and witness the rough justice meted out for petty crime in the last century. Eight Bridewells were built in Kerry in the early nineteenth century – each a self-contained criminal justice unit dealing only in petty crime; with cells, exercise yards, magistrates' court and the keeper's family residence upstairs. Tarbert's restored Bridewell is a gem of its kind and a tribute to community enterprise. Between April and October, the visitor can become involved in one Thomas Dillon's trial for trespass, in the midst of life-size figures and authentic sound.

It is almost a relief to emerge into today's Tarbert – free – having escaped possible transportation to Australia for stealing a sheep or a few hens!

CARRIGAFOYLE CASTLE

Carrigafoyle Castle,a fifteenth century tower house, was the seat of The O'Connor Kerry until 1666, when together with its estates it was confiscated by the British and conferred on Trinity College, Dublin by an Act of Settlement.* It still stands proudly on Shannon's shore two miles north of Ballylongford in North Kerry. Carrig Island shields it from the mouth of the Shannon as it overlooks the Clare coastline across the river. An earlier castle was built here in the 1300s. Tower Houses were very popular in Ireland in the fifteenth and sixteenth centuries and, inside 'The Pale' [Dublin City and its surrounding area] building a Tower House merited a £10 government grant. Self-sufficiency and security were the key features of what were essentially fortified homes, necessary in an era of turbulence, insurrection and reprisal. Hostages were never taken – so it would seem.

It was Cromwell in 1649 who finally brought about the defeat of O'Connor Kerry when one of his battalions captured the castle. O'Connor escaped to Austria. Five men, six women and one child were found hanged inside the castle walls. Even the small limestones, which form the walls of Carrigafoyle castle, seem to exhale the

*It is interesting to note that three centuries later, Brendan Kennelly from up the road in Ballylongford, graduated from Trinity, became one of Ireland's most prestigious poets and now holds the Seat of Modern English in the college.

turbulence and violence of many centuries during which the onslaughts of conquering forces were the order of the day throughout the Irish countryside.

It was *de rigour* for Tower Houses to have a murdering hole through which they could fire on their enemies, and a secret chamber in which, presumably, to hide. A Spanish agent wrote to Philip II of Spain in 1579: 'every petty gentleman lives in a stone tower where he gathers into his services all the rascals of the neighbourhood.' Nevertheless, on 28 March 1580, it was a garrison comprising eighteen Spaniards and fifty Irishmen under the command of an Italian Captain Julio that defended Carrigafoyle Castle from a cannon bombardment by the forces of Sir Pelham and Admiral Winter, which lasted six hours. Not even the surrounding Barbican wall saved the defenders of the castle. On 29 March 1580, Palm Sunday, the wall was breached and all within captured or slain. The prisoners were all hanged off the trees in Killelton, opposite the castle.

On adjacent Carrig Island, treasure abounds in stone and artifact. Its centuries old oyster-fishing has recently been given a new lease of life. Fact is mixed with fiction in countless stories including that of the Colleen Bawn.

One of Carrigafoyle's most talked of visitors in the twentieth century was a cow who made her way up all 104 steps to the top, fell down into the next floor, and had to be carried all the way down again, unscathed, on a mattress!

LISTOWEL CASTLE

Listowel Castle, now a ruin, was a major seat of the Fitz-maurices – Lords of Kerry. Situated on the banks of the River Feale, it marks the southern boundary of the Barony of Irachticonner, one of Kerry's nine baronies. The River Shannon to the north and west, and Tarbert to the east, where it merges into County Limerick, form the remaining borders. Although a ruin, the castle nevertheless has a pleasant aspect as it looks out over Listowel's spacious square. A mix of fact and fiction, or at least legend, is plentifully available to describe its chequered history.

The story of its beginnings is dependent on local tradition. According to J. Anthony Gaughan in his book *Listowel and its Vicinity*, a man named McElligott was the builder and it is his features that are chiselled on a stone that protrudes from the front battlement. Gaughan continues: 'McElligott is the Irish form of Fitzelias of Galway, whose daughter Elena was married to Maurice Fitz-Thomas, and Listowel Castle would have formed part of the marriage settlement.'

Two architectural features are worthy of note. The unusual one is of two turrets joined, a feature shared with Bunratty Castle in County Clare. The other feature, the sculptured head, is thought by some to represent an ape rather than a person. Credence can be given to this if one believes the legend relating to Maurice's second cousin, Tomás an Ápa, father of the first Earl of Desmond. After the Battle of Callan in 1261, an ape who was a household pet cared for Tomás. There are other legends. Only the protruding stone with its sculpted head holds the secret.

The Fitzmaurice family began what was to be a long association with Listowel Castle at the end of the thirteenth century. Although the principal family seats were at Ardfert and Lixnaw, Listowel was of tremendous strategic importance to them. They were constantly feuding, not only with their neighbours, the Desmonds and the O'Neills, but also with the crown forces. Since Listowel Castle was built on the north bank of the River Feale, where the river could be forded, it provided a stronghold to control the movements of visiting would-be marauders across the Feale.

For three centuries, the Lords of Kerry were in constant friction with both their Irish and Anglo-Irish neighbours. The English crown ignored them all, happy to accept only nominal allegiance. But the end came on 5 November 1600, when, after centuries of turmoil, the castle fell to an English force under the command of Sir Charles Wilmot after a 28-day siege. When the castle fell, a village began. It later grew into a town – Listowel town.

St John's Listowel

St John's is a dynamic Theatre and Arts Centre which presides over the old Norman Square of the busy market town of Listowel and its largely agricultural hinterland.

Built in 1819 to a design by Cork architect James Payne, this gothic style stone building served the local Church of Ireland congregation for many generations. Bryan McMahon would tell the story of how on Sunday mornings, before Independence, a platoon of British soldiers billeted on the banks of the River Feale would march up the hill to attend service in St John's, with a few breaking away to go to Mass in St Mary's.

While growing up in Duagh, famous playwright George Fitzmaurice attended service in St John's, conducted by his father. And, more recently, during its restoration period, Ted Hughes, who was later to become Poet Laureate to Queen Elizabeth of England, read his poetry there.

Now, St John's is the mecca for a wide variety of cultural activities in an area already renowned for its writers. New life was breathed into the old grey stone when it was officially opened in 1990, having been restored and refurbished by a voluntary committee. Stained glass windows are complemented by the restful blue furnishings in the auditorium where adaptable seating and lighting provide a flexible space to suit a variety of artistic activities. Local, national and visiting companies from abroad provide theatre in its many forms. Such is their appreciation of the venue that return visits have almost become the norm.

Ever since Listowel recorded and forwarded its condolences to Warrington in Britain after the IRA's tragic bombing of that city, a Warrington Company makes frequent return visits.

St John's Youth Theatre has developed along the way and approximately a hundred children benefit from regular teaching in different art forms. The annual Summer School is a highlight.

The visual arts find a warm welcome, while music in all of its infinite variety can be heard – in fact, St John's is fast developing a high profile for World Music.

Bíonn ranganna Ghaeilge agus dramaí mar ghnáthchuid den chlár.

A tourist information outlet is accommodated in the foyer during the summer months.

BOB BOLAND
POET FARMER

Bob Boland was christened Michael Valentine Boland at his birth in Farranstack in North Kerry – the year was 1888. Everyone knew him quite simply and affectionately as Bob. But, on becoming adept at rhyming and acting with his local group, The Hillside Players, the poet conferred on himself the mock ascendancy title of 'Sir Robert Leslie Boland Bart' – Bart to indicate 'Baronet' no less. His seat of power and influence was a nice cosy farm at Farranstack near Lisselton. His relative, poet Brendan Kennelly, says 'Like all my brothers and sisters, I always called him "Uncle Bob".'

Call him by whatever name one chooses, one thing is certain: this unusual man entertained the population of a couple of Kerry baronies over a few decades during the first half of the century – and he did it in verse! The Mercier Press publication, *Thistles and Docks*, illustrates the wide variety of Boland's poems whose subject matter ranges from honey bees through cow dung, the spud (a sonnet which was broadcast over the BBC), not to mention of course, adventures with an enema, whilst a patient in a Dublin hospital. This latter is actually titled 'Adventure with Nurse Doyle'. In it he describes how his nurse attempted to pass the enema tube:

> *And at one end (it could be seen)*
> *'Twas buttered o'er with Vaseline;*
> *And this was done to lubricate*
> *Each moving part; to eliminate*
> *Stern friction's law and so make smooth*
> *The passage of this demon tube.*
> *She raised the clothes, I did not stir,*
> *But let my arse grin out at her ...*

And it goes on and on to a final successful ending, after many fits and starts!

In *Thistles and Docks,* the publisher divides the different subjects under separate titles. One such section called 'Poetic Justice' contains what surely must be a unique exchange in verse between the defendant, to wit Robert Boland, and the District Justice, R. D. F. Johnson, himself no mean playwright. Our poet was summoned to Castleisland Court in November 1949 to defend three summonses for not having wings, tax or insurance on his lorry at Castleisland Fair. He penned a poem to Justice Johnson:

> *Wishing not to offend,*
> *Being too far to attend*
> *Hence, by proxy defend*
> *With the Muse (my old friend).*
> *You know that a lorry*
> *Is a deep source of worry*
> *With the tax and insurance*
> *And driving endurance;*
> *Wings rusting and breaking;*
> *Lads stealing or taking*

Our tax – could you bate 'em!
From the mirror bar swinging,
Shouting and singing,
Pulled its bolts through the tin, in
The cab at Listowel.

Bob goes on to explain how he did not have time to do repairs before Castleisland Fair and how the gardaí summonsed him. He finishes with subtle and roguish pleas:

Perhaps make the fine small
Maybe no fine at all?
This last line I withdraw.
You knowing well the Law
And a good Justice must
Dispense Justice that's just.
Now, reflecting on this,
May be wrong to dismiss –
Less along this crude rhyme,
Might absolve me in time?

Well, District Justice Johnson could not resist this poetic plea and dismissed the case, also in verse! His reply and much more can be found in Bob Boland's *Thistles and Docks*.

LARTIGUE RAILWAY

In February 1888, a unique railway line, using a single elevated rail system, was formally opened in Listowel, Its function was to provide a rail service between Listowel and Ballybunion, nine miles away, with a stop in Lisselton. The service continued until 1924 and became known by railway enthusiasts world-wide for its singular monorail, which was invented by a Frenchman with a Spanish name, Francoise Lartigue. On that February day in 1888, French and German could be heard mingling with the Kerry accents, so great was the continental interest in the new rail phenomenon, to be known forever as The Lartigue Railway.

Francoise Lartigue found inspiration for his invention in Algeria in 1881, while observing a camel train in the desert. Loads were carried pannier-style on either side of each camel. He saw the camels' legs as trestles with their bodies providing the driving power.

After various experiments with other sources of power, he finally patented a steam engine for the Lartigue Railway which, for 36 years, was to provide the only public transport between Listowel and the seaside resort of Ballybunion. Farmers through whose land the railway went used specially designed elevated crossings over the track.

The carriages on the Lartigue boasted three classes –

first class, a curious combination of first and second class and a third class. On occasion, when the engine failed to pull the train up Gortnaskeha Height near Ballybunion, first class passengers were advised to stay put, second class to alight and walk, while the third class passengers were told to get out and push!

Balance was an important factor of the Lartigue Railway – passengers providing some, while rolling-stock freight was also used on occasion.

Local comedian John Leslie rhymed:

> *The old train's held together with rope*
> *And the tackling they say won't endure Sir*
> *Sure they balance the people with soap*
> *And sometimes with bags of manure Sir!*

In 1988, a Listowel committee led by Michael Guerin, worked on a centenary project. This culminated in a well-researched book and a built-to-scale model of a unique rail system, which may be viewed in Listowel's Public Library.

At the time of writing a committee, chaired by Jack McKenna of Listowel, is working on the restoration of the Lartigue Railway.

BALLYBUNION

'You can't beat the Ballybunion air!' This is probably the greatest compliment the annual holidaymaker can give on arrival at the magnificent strip of North Kerry coastline where, as the song says, 'The Shannon River meets the sea'. Ballybunion is named after the Bunyan family who, in 1582, acquired the fourteenth-century castle on the green. Hence the name Castle Green for the small promontory on which the ruined remains appear to acknowledge the winking light of the Loop Head lighthouse, Ceann Léime, across in County Clare. The latter seems to guide the Shannon around the head to where it joins the Atlantic swell. To the south and west, the River Cashen, well known for its salmon fishing, joins the sea against the boundary of Kerry Head with peaks of the Sliabh Mish mountain range visible on a clear day.

At low tide, the 4.5-mile (7km) walk from the Castle Green through the Men's Strand, to the Cashen, along a wonderful stretch of sandy beach, is more than amply repaid by visual excitement. Sea, river and sky surround a colourful coastline. Bird life includes feeding seabirds – sandpipers, oyster-catchers and plovers to name but a few. High on the cliff on the left, golfers from here and from many lands can be seen silhouetted against the sky as they play the internationally renowned golf links.

Going left into the sand dunes a cormorant or a

heron may come into view while on Ballyeigh Strand, down from the Cashen car park, fishermen land a salmon catch from their ganlows. The gondolas used by the British gentry visiting Lixnaw Castle in the fourteenth and fifteenth centuries inspired the design for these boats. Visiting ladies enjoyed pleasure trips up and down the Cashen in the original gondolas. For today's walker, a choice of beach or road can be made for the return journey to the Castle Green.

There are many rambles round Ballybunion and a booklet of that name, written by Keith and Veronica Long, is available locally. It features inland and hill walks, a cycle and the spectacular cliff walk, which begins over Ladies Strand on the northern side of the Castle Green. Swimmers, surfers, walkers, cyclists and golfers frequently end their activities by taking a hot seaweed bath on the ladies' beach, followed by delicious hot buttered scones and tea, while gazing out over the Atlantic breakers.

BALLYHEIGUE

Ballyheigue is widely regarded as being one of North Kerry's most popular family seaside resorts. A ninth-century ruler of the O'Connor Clan, Tadhg, is said to have given the parish its name. A fin-shaped entrance to the village allows the roads from Tralee and Shannonside to converge and form one main street leading straight to the village, towards the Atlantic Ocean and America, which Ballyheigue claims as its next parish! One can have fantastic mirages to support this claim by standing on the Kerry Head promontory under whose sheltering crook the village nestles, gazing out towards the distant Atlantic horizon.

Indeed, with the lordly Shannon and the majestic Atlantic surrounding the parish on three sides, sea and sky-scapes ensure endless visual delights. Tralee Bay provides a cosy, sandy cove for the beach, where the eye is taken upwards towards the gentle slopes of the Sliabh Mish mountain range, ending with Brandon Head standing sentinel over the sea. Carlisle's *Dictionary* of 1807 says simply that Ballyheigue is a place 'situate upon the Atlantic Ocean'.

A statue of Roger Casement points towards a car park and promenade leading to five miles of safe, sandy beach which gives a summer focus to the south side. In the distance, the Black Rock beckons the walker and a great variety of bird life is reward at journey's end.

Ruined remains of the nineteenth century Crosby Castle dominate the promontory on the approach to the spectacular Kerry Head walk. The Crosbys, in time of financial need, resorted to smuggling in an ideally suited strip of coastline abounding in caves. A golf course now surrounds the castle. Famous residents of Ballyheigue included writer Christy Browne, of *My Left Foot*, book and film, fame.

More recently, a huge whale found beached continues to be a source of wonder. Its skeleton is the centrepiece of Ballyheigue's maritime museum.

THE NORTH KERRY MUSEUM

The North Kerry Museum incorporates under its all-embracing roof, a heritage and environmental centre. The museum is easy to find. From north Kerry, a road from Tarbert's ferry port leads to the museum through Ballybunion or Listowel – in either case taking the Ballyduff Road over the Ferry Bridge. From south and east Kerry, the road through Tralee to Ballyduff leads there. The museum is set in a landscape that is patterned with antiquities and overlooks the River Cashen with Ballyeigh Strand beyond – Ballyeigh of nineteenth century faction-fight memory.

The museum breathes history. On entering, a mediaeval type armchair of regal design greets the visitor. It was such a chair, made for the nineteenth century gentry's carriages, on which Lord Kitchener's pregnant mother sat while journeying from Gunnsborough outside Listowel. *En route*, a sudden onset of labour caused Kitchener Junior to be born in a shed at the back of a crofter's cottage.

Guided by the dynamic curator, Seán Quinlan, every object in the museum comes alive. Panels painted mural-style on the walls illustrate the crests of Kerry's ancient noble families. Below them is evidence of fame and famine as centuries of history unfold through hundreds of artifacts. A huge famine soup pot, with a long wooden stirring implement, stands as a searing indictment of how a conqueror's indifference brought a proud race to its knees only about 150 years ago.

Upstairs not even the charming river and sandscapes framed in the window succeed in distracting visitors from a continuing walk through history. What did she look like – the lady who wore that dainty deerskin shoe at a time when a high king ruled Ireland a thousand years ago? And there is much evidence of wine-smuggling at the nearby caves in Meenagohane. Did some of the Spanish sailors decide to settle on that rough, rocky, beautiful coastline as they bargained with the Kerry smugglers?

An open display tests every visitor's honesty. Did anything ever go missing? Yes. One woodbine cigarette from a very old wild woodbine pack. A small boy helped himself to a woodbine, went outside, smoked it, got sick, came back and confessed! There are special entry rates for children and families, and easy access welcomes all comers. The disabled are free of charge – which includes all disability. A wheelchair at the ready ensures that nobody is excluded. 'And,' says Seán Quinlan, as he returns to his research for the *Great Book of Kerry – A history of the County from 10,000 BC to modern times* – 'sure if anyone needed a cup of tea, you couldn't refuse 'em. Charge 'em? Not at all.'

Ardfert Cathedral
Hostage to Fortune

Ardfert cathedral and abbey dominate a fertile valley about six miles north of Tralee. The mix of architectural styles and masonry are indicative of centuries-old religious vibrancy when Ardfert remained unchallenged as the Episcopal See of Kerry. Tradition has it that in the fifth century Saint Brendan was guided to the site by a bird and founded his first monastery there. His teacher, Bishop Erc, was the first bishop of Ardfert and carried responsibility for the faithful of Kerry.

Evidence of some of the finest historic ecclesiastical buildings in Ireland still remains. Saint Brendan's first monastery is, of course, long gone, but many others replaced it down through the centuries. A friary quickly followed the cathedral; a round tower to the south-west was blown down in an eighteenth century storm. Records remain of Ardfert castle, Glandore Gate, Ardfert Parish Rooms and The Fountain.

The south transept of the cathedral is now in a pristine state of recent renovation but the ruins generally are still in a good state of preservation. The three elegant painted windows in the eastern front are strikingly beautiful and find an architectural counterpoint in the four round arches on the western front. Indeed the cathedral site with its two adjacent churches illustrates Irish church architecture during one of the finest periods. The size of the cathedral also indicates a well-populated area.

For five hundred years after Bishop Erc, with a couple of exceptions in episcopal terms, Kerry carried the title: Diocese of Ardfert. In its ability to survive, this religious building complex epitomises the spirit of the old Roman Catholic hymn, 'Faith of our Fathers', since much of it still remains 'in spite of dungeon, fire and sword'. Over the centuries, it was pillaged; devastated, struck by lightning and suffered many episcopal disputes. The pope had to intervene on a number of occasions when the Anglo-Romans arrived in north Kerry and sought to appoint their own bishops. Despite upheavals and disputes, in fairness to the feuding ecclesiastics – they did prioritise their architecture!

No less than three religious orders arrived in Ardfert during the end of the thirteenth and the beginning of the fourteenth centuries: Dominicans, Franciscans and Cistercians. Ardfert town flourished and during the Middle Ages it became one of the three most important towns in Kerry, the other two being Dingle and Tralee. The Fitzmaurice family who were Lords of Kerry for 400 years, from the thirteenth to the seventeenth centuries, chose Ardfert as their main seat of power. They would seem to have been a benign force in the area; they built a house for lepers and a Franciscan friary.

The Crosby family took over from the Fitzmaurices

during the seventeenth century after the Plantation of Munster. John Crosby was appointed the first Protestant Bishop of Ardfert. And in 1671, Ardfert cathedral was extended and converted into a Protestant church. Subsequently, the Church of Ireland Bishopric assumed the title of Limerick, Ardfert and Aghadoe.

Church of Ireland authority in the area waned during the early nineteenth century. A Roman Catholic bishop, Bishop Egan, was appointed bishop of all of Kerry. It took until the 1930s before the Diocese of Kerry was finally, and canonically, accepted.

Racing in Kerry

You will find a race-meeting in Kerry each month from April to September. Killarney eases us into the first summer meeting in May and celebrates high summer with a repeat in July. In Killarney, you can mix breathtaking scenery with your gambling. Sometimes, the mist-covered mountains seem to form a neo-impressionist backdrop to the enclosure. When the sun breaks through wonderful blues and purples peep through the mist to bewitch and dazzle.

Tralee, our capital town, invites you to have your first seasonal flutter on the June bank holiday weekend. Having made everything ready for the off, the Ballybeggan course emerges in full colour for six days in August. The complementary Rose of Tralee Festival tinges everything with all the colours of the rainbow, when streets, parks and pubs reflect an international carnival atmosphere that spills over onto the racing enclosure.

Indeed, colour is an inherent part of every race-meeting. The jockeys' colours or silks make their own statement to many people – my mother was one of these. She would talk of going by train from Tralee to Listowel for the Harvest Festival meeting, all decked out in hat and gloves. She had an easy way of picking winners. She would study the line-up of horses in the parade ring before each race. Her observations did not include either the form or the appearance of the horses. No! She would give careful consideration to the jockey's colours. The jockey's cap was the final decider; if it topped the total look of horse and rider with style, then that was her certainty.

An old man remembers when he was a small boy of eight, in a grey gansey, wearing no shoes and sporting smackers, a close-cut hairstyle with a front fringe peculiar to small boys in those days, he first went racing to the Island in 1926. At eight years of age you didn't have to pay into the races, provided you attached yourself to a willing adult with the simple request: 'can I come in with you?'

On the first day of Listowel Races in the autumn of 1926, a tick tack man in the stand enclosure signalled to the bookies outside – 'Court Picture ridden by Joe Canty would win the next race'. The small boy put down his sixpence. He never saw the race; couldn't leave the bookie's side. You could not take the chance, if the horse won, the bookie might take off with your winnings! Nowadays bookies are very solid members of society but, in the early part of the last century, it wasn't un-known in Listowel for a bookie who, finding himself with too much to pay out, would leg it off across the Island in his bowler hat – with betting tickets falling out of his leather bag and fellows flying after him to kill him!

The six-day Listowel meeting has its origins way back in the last century. Its festival atmosphere is both folk memory and present reality. The Island racecourse is famed in song and story. The attendant festival with its street music and competitions adds to the atmosphere. But, the race-meeting, with its vast attendance and record-breaking gambling is paramount.

The great thing about all our race-meetings is that you can quite happily go on your own. Friends and kindred spirits are never difficult to find. In fact, between the chat, the odd jar, and the camaraderie, sometimes you would almost forget to back the winner of the next race!

Some Personal Memoirs of
Joan Collis Sandes

Like all old 'big houses', Oak Park, which now has a whole area in a Tralee suburb called after it, has many stories to tell. But since bricks and mortar can only give mute evidence of what shapes people's lives, a human voice is the only conduit through which the atmosphere of a time or place can subsequently come alive, provided of course memoirs are made and kept. Luckily, one of the Collis Sandes family, whose home Oak Park was – and after whose family name the house is now known – 'jotted down things' as she describes it. Joan Collis Sandes describes the old lovely house in which she grew up: 'Oak Park was a roomy house with a central hall going up to the roof, with a gallery round two sides.'

Her description of the house-lighting as it was, and the difference the advent of proper light made, tells its own story. Its entire source of light was a hanging Italian brass lamp with another against the stairs. 'When we went to bed we took a candle in a silver stick, lighting two more in our bedrooms when we got there. This was quite normal lighting and one read happily in bed by one candlelight! When I was eighteen in 1907, we put in acetylene gas, a very pretty, soft, good, light which would be run into standard lamps – and transformed life. Each light had to be lit by a taper. William stayed up until the ladies went to bed and then put them out. "Will I quench the lights now?" was his expression.'

They never put out the light in those days, always 'quenched' it. And, referring to tea, they never 'made' tea, always 'wetted' it! In the happy, privileged world that was Oak Park, the lady remembers with almost casual recall 'I never remember any paper money below a £5 note. Before the First World War, we sailed around Europe with fat golden sovereigns and real silver change'. Miss Collis Sandes, like every young woman of her class, travelled 'with a sporran-like bag under your petticoat pinned to the corset, containing all your excess money, travellers cheques and jewellery'. Once her sister Margaret, 'after retirement for research work' – which of course meant unpinning the sporran from its place of concealment, 'was able to pour out the required sovereigns to pay for an unplanned train journey – which made her feel very capable!'

Irish trains apparently had no heating until the First World War. 'They flung,' our traveller recalls, 'leaky, tepid but steaming metal foot warmers into the carriage – the steam soon had you damp to the knees'. But, 'the food in restaurant cars was your glory on your way back from school in England. The crossing well over – 6.15 am and Dublin only beginning to stir – the usual head waiter to welcome you and the glory of omelettes, bacon, tomatoes, hot toast and marmalade before you'.

Kerry was fortunate of course to be served by the

Great Southern Railway – the best in Ireland – because of the tourist traffic going south. In 1912, the Collis Sandes family changed from horse-drawn transport to a Ford car – 'a tin lizzie with the minimum of works'. Not only did the horses on the road go hysterical at the sound of the horn but, sometimes, also the people themselves

Oak Park later served as a noviciate for the Presentation Sisters, was owned by the Department of Agriculture, and is now open for community purposes.

GOING TO THE DOGS

'Your man is gone to the dogs' said in a certain way, carries more than a hint of youth being misspent or of early middle age dissipation. But, 'Are you going to the dogs tonight?' implies a different thing entirely. The 'dogs' in question are greyhounds – a breed of canine much beloved of Kerry people for many generations. An early image of greyhound owners is of seriously healthy-looking men in peaked caps and wellingtons or strong boots, 'walking dogs' as they put it, round the streets and roads of our towns and countryside. So much in public evidence were the men with greyhounds on leather leashes, that Bryan MacMahon remarked to me once, and with some amusement, 'There was an American visiting me last week and he asked me "Say, does everybody in Ireland walk whippets?"'

Women adopted the greyhound industry also and have assumed equal partnership with their men folk. A fascinating industry grew around their breeding, training, racing and exporting. Racing tracks opened in the 1920s, including one in Ardfert in 1929. Ballybunion followed suit. But it is Tralee that has given the most consistent commitment to greyhound racing in Kerry, beginning with the establishment in 1930 of the Kingdom Greyhound Racing Company. This company's brief was to facilitate the sport at Oakview Park situated in a 7.5-acre site in Tralee's northern suburbs. Facilities for owners and dogs have been upgraded over the years, culminating in the opening of a splendid multi-purpose grandstand on 1 June 1997.

In the Weighing Room a few yards from the stand, each dog is weighed under the supervision of steward Frank Thornton with manager John Ward always visible. Here, accents of owners and trainers blend with great good humour – from the soft English vowels of Olive Kelly from Knocknagoshel to the real Kerry of Lyrecrompane's Billy McCarthy. Stepping into the ground floor concourse of the new grandstand, a smart college atrium comes to mind, with soft light and decor, quick food and drink, round tables and discreet tote facilities. For the more traditional punter, the bookies are arranged out front.

Michael Field, Managing Director of Ireland's Racetracks for Bord na gCon, repeated a recently overheard remark while noting the ever-increasing number of glamourous patrons at the Tralee track, 'one time everyone wore spectacles in the stand – now all you see is young wans and glamour'!

Should you ignore the lift, walking upstairs ensures an excellent view of Renee Kennelly's artistic depiction of a gleaming greyhound. This artist is also responsible for the general décor. The superb view from the glassed-in restaurant and bar looks over Traps, Track and Winning Post, and the Sliabh Mish mountains beckon to the right.

'Going to the dogs' has taken on a whole new dimension in Kerry.

SIAMSA TÍRE
THE NATIONAL FOLK THEATRE OF IRELAND

Siamsa Tíre attracts thousands of visitors each year to its state of the art theatre in Tralee.

Small beginnings with a church choir, which began to experiment in the 1960s with music, song and dance in the Irish folk idiom, gradually led to the formation of a full-blown theatre company – now experienced, confident and sophisticated. The director of that early 1960s choir was Fr Pat Ahern.

Subsequently, his enthusiasm led him on a personal crusade to foster Irish dance steps and teach them to young enthusiasts; this devotion to the dance came to be the badge of Siamsa Tíre. A North Kerry dance teacher, Jerry 'Munnix' Molyneaux, was the source from which this sparkling river of accomplishment flowed.

Now, Siamsa Tíre entertains audiences from virtually all corners of the globe during its annual six-month season of folk theatre presentations in Tralee, and regularly travels abroad to represent Ireland at high-profile events. Two rural training centres, Teach Siamsa in Finuge near Listowel *agus ceann eile i gceart lár na Gaeltachta taobh le Séipéal na Carraige,* introduce many young people to what is now the Siamsa Tíre tradition.

Siamsa Tíre continues to experiment with many formats, blending myth, legend and folklore into modern theatrical presentations. Directors, designers and choreographers from other traditions are invited to participate from time to time. The ancient ring fort design of Siamsa Tíre also incorporates an exciting Arts Centre. External professional, amateur and community companies are warmly welcomed into this lovely centre for all the arts – theatre, music, song, dance and the visual arts. Art exhibitions change regularly, and the centre, through its innovative programming policy, provides a diverse mix of professional and community arts, education, training and development for the south-west region.

THE ROSE OF TRALEE

Though lovely and fair as the rose of the summer
Yet t'was not her beauty alone that won me
Oh no, t'was the truth in her eyes ever dawning
That made me love Mary the Rose of Tralee.

This verse written in the mid-nineteenth century is part of a now internationally famous song and the inspiration for the annual festival held in Tralee at the end of August.

The words of 'The Rose of Tralee' are widely attributed to William Pembroke Mulchinock who came from a wealthy Tralee merchant family. He lived in Big House style in West Villa, Ballyard – a still fashionable suburb of Tralee.

By contrast, Mary O'Connor, the beautiful subject of the song, was brought up at the other end of the social and material scale in Brogue Lane, where Rock Street is now. Brogue Lane, as the name implies, was devoted to boot-making. The powerful middle-class families of which Mulchinock was part were scarcely aware of its existence.

But, Mary O'Connor became nursemaid to William Mulchinock's little nieces at West Villa. And, it was in the nursery of the Big House that the ill-fated love-story began when our hero came to visit his nieces and clapped eyes on Mary for the first time.

After that meeting, the pair became inseparable. Family and society frowned but to no avail. On the evening of their betrothal, Willie was sought by the police to be arrested for a murder committed during a Daniel O'Connell meeting held in Tralee that day. Although innocent of the crime, he was encouraged to flee to India where he worked as a war correspondent.

His return to Tralee to be reunited with Mary tragically coincided with her death. William Mulchinock later made an unhappy marriage and went to live in America working as a journalist and writing poetry. He returned alone to Tralee a broken man and died in October 1864, aged forty-four. He is buried beside his lovely Mary, the first Rose of Tralee.

CRAG CAVES

And the waters murmuring
With such consort as they keep
Entice the dewy-feather'd sleep
And let some strange mysterious dream
Wave at his wings in airy stream …

These lines taken from John Milton's seventeenth century poem *Il Penseroso* are somewhat reflective of the atmosphere to be experienced in Crag Cave near Castleisland. This extraordinary cave is thought to date back 400 million years, give or take a million years or two. In fact, Crag Cave could have been a positive impulse in the Creator's thought processes during those first six days of creation!

But it was during the seventh day of creation, a mere one and a half million years ago, that a warming climate heralded the most recent meltdown in our history. The ensuing surface water then trickled through cave ceilings made of limestone rock, to form underground streams; these in turn caused the formation of underground caves and caverns through erosion and saturation. Crag Cave is a wonderful example of how nature's magical fantasies can literally form an underground theatre with spaces for all manner of performance.

To the Geaney family, on whose land this natural wonder became evident, goes the credit for actively encouraging the assessment and development of the project and for ultimately realising what began as a dream. During the 1980s all manner of experts, including geologists and cave engineers, were invited to conduct a survey and to report back. These included John Crichton of Marble Arch Caves who concluded: 'At Castleisland, Co. Kerry, there exists a cave of exceptional interest, quality and beauty … exquisitely attractive and abundantly decorated with calcite formations, not available elsewhere on the scale available in Crag Cave'.

Dan Walsh of Castleisland pioneered the excavation of the main shaft in 1987. To experienced Speleologist, Brian Judd, was given the responsibility for making the cave both safe and attractive for visitors of all ages. His team included Denis Barry, Denis Leen and Pat Nolan.

Academics, Professor John Gunn and Brigid Scanlon, gave the benefit of their experience. Welsh cave diver, Martyn Farr, found a cave 'measureless to man'. Fellow cave diver, John Cooper, and the rest of the team – apparently undaunted – soon joined forces with him.

Within two days, and having surveyed 1,670 metres, such was the magic of the newly discovered chamber and passages that an extraordinary christening suggested itself. Where else might more appropriate names be found other than in J. R. R. Tolkien's book, *Lord of the Rings*! So, prompted by Michael Scott's theatrical lighting, you emerge through Aerobes Ecstasy to Minas Tirith and on and on through an exotic subterranean world where echoes of the famous Diarmuid and Gráinne love story catch the imagination, in a pre-historic world where stalactites, stalagmites and pillars form the décor of a natural wonderland.

BLENNERVILLE

Blennerville is a charming village about one mile from Tralee, due west along the Dingle Road. Sir Rowland Blennerhassett developed the village in the eighteenth century. And, presumably, to provide an industrial base for the village, he built a quay nearby on the shores of Tralee Bay from which to export the stone-ground flour produced by his third project, a 60ft high windmill.

Blennerville prospered during the Napoleonic Wars, when flour was in short supply on the continent; it also found markets in Britain. In those days, production often reached five tons of flour per week.

Blennerville Windmill closed in the 1880s due to a combination of factors, including the loss of exports because of the opening of the Tralee Ship Canal and the introduction of the steam-driven engine. This was to make the wind and water driven engines in Western Europe defunct.

In the 1980s the by now ruined windmill required a decision by the Local Authority, Tralee Urban District Council, as to whether it should be restored or demolished. In 1984, a combination of statutory and voluntary forces decided on the former. Now the Windmill at Blennerville surveys the sea and countryside in all its former glory and holds within its ambit a large visitor centre, craft workshops and a restaurant.

Nearby, part of the old reconstructed Tralee/Dingle Steam Railway plies its business between Tralee and Blennerville on its narrow-gauge line, providing a nostalgic trip back in time's whirligig for the rail enthusiast, and much wonderment for children. But the realisation of even more of Blennerville's former glory is envisaged. To further complement Windmill and Steam train, a re-creation of a mid nineteenth century sailing ship – the *Jeanie Johnston* is complete. During the Famine of the mid 1840s, the original gallant *Jeanie Johnston* brought thousands of young Irish emigrants to safe harbour in America – never losing a passenger!

God blessed all who sailed in her. May He do so again!

CASTLEGREGORY

Between 1891 and 1939, it was possible to travel to Castlegregory on the Tralee to Dingle Railway. Apart from the spectacular scenery *en route,* the Tralee–Dingle narrow gauge line was famous for adventurous travel. Once, in 1893, a 'pig special' was derailed and went over Curraduff Bridge in Camp. This resulted in a travel-writer advising travellers to Dingle to take the branch line to Castlegregory and thence over Conor Hill – walking one presumes! Some years later, the train was actually blown off the tracks in a gale. The number of stations that were serviced between Tralee and Castlegregory, suggests a city bus route of today. There were eight stops after Tralee: The Basin, Blennerville, Curraheen, Derrymore, Camp Junction, Deelish, Aughcashla and Castlegregory.

Although now without any trace of the castle that gave it its name, Castlegregory is situated as it is between Tralee Bay and Brandon Bay. A road north leads to a narrow strip of land and the Maherees – where there are accessible islands, beautiful beaches and wonderful scenery everywhere.

There are two claimants to the origins of the village's name – one of whom is Pope Gregory the Great who, although well-in with the English was well-liked in Ireland. He was known as Gregory Goldenmouth and claimed to be from Corca Dhuibhne. John Millington Synge refers to 'the boy Gregory of the Goldenmouth' in his play *Riders to the Sea.* Perhaps Kerry can claim a pope among its native sons!

A Romeo and Juliet inference in the second suggested origin of Castlegregory's name has all the romance and tragedy of Shakespeare's play. A Gregory Hoare built the castle in the mid sixteenth century. He and a neighbour called Moore were constantly feuding. Old Gregory actually took a fit and died when his son Hugh married Moore's daughter in 1566.

Over a dozen years later Lord Grey's army elected to stay in Hoare's Castle on their way to Smerwick. Hugh Hoare's wife emptied all the wine barrels rather than show hospitality to the queen's men. Her husband Hugh stabbed her to death in a rage and died suddenly himself the next day.

Due to various political reasons, the castle came to be unfavourably regarded. Its stone walls were dismantled and used to build houses in the village. Not a trace of it remains. For all that, from the village itself and all through to the Maherees, this beautiful sea-locked neck of land remains steeped in history with obvious evidence everywhere – significant stones, the odd shipwreck, a Harry Clarke stained glass window in the Catholic church and, if you're lucky, a glimpse of the black frog, unique in Ireland, to Kerry – the Natterjack Toad.

DINGLE

Ever since the fourteenth century, Dingle has remained the principal harbour of the magnificent peninsula of Corca Dhuibhne – a barony in its own right. Like the rest of the Kerry coast, merchants from Spain and other countries plied their trade here. Records show that some of them settled in Dingle. Specific Spanish influences were evident in the early architecture of Dingle town as it grew around an increasingly important trading port. Even its very first pier, made of wood, was known as the Spanish Pier.

Ships from Portugal, Spain, France and Britain exchanged fine wines and other merchandise for the locally produced wool and hides. The inept reign of Edward II brought political confusion in both Britain and Ireland. Middle-class bigotry peaked and the serfs were kept firmly in bondage, although they did free themselves sufficiently to become tenants of their lords and masters. These serfs, *na brataigh*, did not become legally free until the seventeenth century. Despite the imbalances of local society, Dingle and Tralee were thriving towns in the fourteenth century. Not even the continuing famine caused by excessive rain or the plague known as the Black Death, which reached parts of Ireland from Britain and Europe, got as far as Dingle.

But unrest continued to be the order of the day. A type of guerrilla warfare was rampant in the country-side. Pleas were made to Spain and other sympathetic countries for help to save Irish Catholicism. Actually, a very successful missionary project to spread Protestant-ism in the nineteenth century was vigorously pursued in Dingle town. Protestant converts even had special houses built for them. The area is known to this day as 'The Colony'. Later in the same century, a counter-movement by the Catholic Church largely reversed the Protestant successes.

Piracy was rampant along the coast and spirits and tobacco smuggling reached a new peak. The local linen industry flourished side by side with piracy. Fine linens became the core business of the town. Sadly it declined towards the end of the fourteenth century.

Now, Dingle is the prosperous head of a thriving peninsula. Harbour development, including a marina, ensures its future as both a fishing port and a centre of maritime leisure. Boat building in Dingle predates St Brendan's time. In recent years a lovely craft, the *St Colmcille*, left the boatyard. Gourmet eating, literature and many arts and crafts including pottery, weaving, silver work and leather and the visual arts have developed side by side.

The friendly dolphin, Fungi, frolics in the harbour. Wildlife champion and filmmaker Eamon de Buitléir said of him: 'One of the most exciting encounters I have had with marine mammals was while filming a dolphin near the mouth of Dingle Harbour'. Thousands of Fungi fans flock to Dingle Harbour to have their own exciting encounters – and he loves them too!

St Brendan

Although St Patrick never came to Kerry, the life and times of St Brendan would indicate that Christianity had reached at least the coastal areas by the end of the fifth century. Visiting Spanish sailors selling wine and other merchandise may well have introduced the message of Christianity and Jesus Christ to ports such as Fenit near Tralee, where Brendan was born in 484.

Ireland was not much documented in the fifth century; it is never easy to separate myth from fact. However, it is generally accepted that Brendan was of noble birth, his parents Finnlug and Cara being descendants of Fergus MacRory, Ireland's high king in the first century. Tradition has it that Bishop Erc, an emissary of St Patrick, founded the Christian community to which they belonged. Amid reported heavenly phenomena, which have been variously interpreted, Brendan was baptised at Tobar na Molt (Wether's Well) near Ardfert. It is thought that Brendan, when just a year old, and following an Irish custom of the time, was fostered out to St Ita at her monastery in Kileedy, Co. Limerick. Back home again he studied scripture, the classics, mathematics and astronomy with Bishop Erc.

Following St Patrick's mission to Ireland, monasteries abounded and were each as self-sufficient as a village or a small town. Each monastery was also the focus of learning and of community life in the district. For young men of Brendan's class it was quite usual to visit such foundations and he followed the pattern as far north as Roscommon. Much later he was again to cross the Shannon to found his famous monastery at Clonfert in East Galway. His religious zeal was evidenced soon after his ordination to the priesthood. Brendan founded Ardfert monastery outside Tralee.

For his personal oratory he chose the summit of Mount Brandon, the highest peak of the Dingle mountain range, which looks majestically down as it sweeps to the Atlantic Ocean. Perhaps it was from the rugged splendour of Mount Brandon that Brendan first became aware of a new continent across the wide Atlantic. But it was while revisiting his most renowned foundation in Clonfert that he heard stories of a new world beyond the western sea. Inspired by these stories he came back to Kerry and, with seven companions, set sail from Brandon Creek on his quest. He was already an accomplished sailor. Did Brendan discover America before either the Vikings or Columbus? Eminent historians of recent times are convinced that he did.

In 1976, Tim Severin reconstructed the boat from a description in a medieval manuscript. He set out with five companions from Brandon Creek and fetched up in Newfoundland thirteen months later, thus making the sixth century story of St Brendan's voyage quite probable.

St Brendan of Kerry and Clonfert died in the convent of his sister Briga, in County Galway in the year 577.

RYAN'S DAUGHTER

At the end of 1968 and through all of 1969, a film was made in the Dingle area of West Kerry that was to change everything, utterly. *Ryan's Daughter,* directed by David Lean and starring Sarah Miles, Robert Mitchum and John Mills, was to be the catalyst that would transform the Dingle Peninsula from wonderful but poor isolation, into a vibrant playground for tourists and artists.

In the film, human passion and breathtaking scenery rival one another for the attention of the audience. Although its location was based primarily in the parish of Dunquin, with its unique view of the Blaskets, *Ryan's Daughter* also includes scenes shot in Barrow, Banna and Inch strands, Killarney, Clare and as far away as Africa. But it was around Dingle and Dunquin that the local economy, hitherto a very depressed economy, showed a sudden, marked improvement. In his book *An Rialtas ab Fhearr! Scannán David Lean – Ryan's Daughter,* Micheál de Mordha describes one of the first encouraging, visible signs. A returning emigrant from America, Maidhc Dainín Ó Sé, now a writer, stopped off on the way home to have a pint in a pub in Dingle. *Lorg sé piont dó féin.* He paid for his pint and noticed as he drank it all the English accents that could be heard among the crowd in the pub. He put up the price of a second pint and the barman shook his head – *'Tá sé ceart go leor; tá sé íochta as cheana féin'* – it's

OK – it's paid for!'

'Who paid for it?'

'Ryan's Daughter', came the answer!

Maidhc looked around the pub to locate this generous woman and to let her know that he was a married man with two children – only to be told that *Ryan's Daughter* was the title name of a film that was being shot in the area. Five pints he drank on *Ryan's Daughter* that day!

During the period of set building and the creation of a whole new village in Dunquin, to be known as Kirrary, every available lodging and house around Dingle was booked or leased. Demand for just about everything reached epic proportions.

Pub grub and prosperity had arrived in West Kerry!

THE BLASKETS

The Blasket Islands are set like jewels in the Atlantic Ocean off the coast of Corca Dhuibhne, the Dingle Peninsula, in West Kerry. Poet Seán Ó Ríordáin recommended that, 'to discover one's true nature, it is necessary to take the coast road to Dún Chaoin'.

On reaching the Point at Slea Head, a breathtaking vista of sea and landscape never fails to stir the senses. The sea is sometimes calm and shimmering in the sunlight and at other times boisterous and defiant. It is always magnificent!

The Ferriter family controlled the Blaskets from the end of the thirteenth century until 1653, when Captain Piaras Feirtéar, poet and rebel chieftain, was defeated at Ross Castle Killarney and hanged at Cnoch na gCaorach nearby. *Is léir go raibh daoine riabh ag cur futha ar na mBlascaoid. Tá a fhios againn gur mhair cúpla teaghlach in Inis Mhic Uibhleán agus Inis Tuaisceart chomh déanach le deireadh an naoú haois déag.* (People always used to live on the Blasket Islands. We know that a couple of families lived on in Inis Mhic Uibhleán and Inis Tuaisceart as late as the nineteenth century).

Now, only Inish Mhic Uibhleán has a sometimes inhabitant – a former Taoiseach Charles J. Haughey.

The hard island life caused the population to decline and in the mid 1950s the Blaskets were finally given back to nature. But not before a unique way of life was re-corded with the encouragement of visiting scholars. The most outstanding of these was the famous Norwegian linguist, Carl Marstrander, a scholar of Old Irish. Mar-strander became known affectionately as *An Lochlannach* – The Viking. And it is he who is credited with instilling esteem for their culture into the Islanders. Marstrander left the Blaskets to teach in Dublin. Soon after he en-couraged one of his students, Robin Flower from the Bri-tish Museum, to perfect his Irish in the Great Blasket. He became known as *Bláithín* – Little Flower. He continued where The Viking left off.

The Islanders began to tell their stories. Peig Sayers told hers in *Peig;* Muiris Ó Súilleabháin his in *Twenty Years A-growing – Fiche Blain ag Fás.* The classic book of the Blaskets is Tomás Ó Criomhthain's, *An tOileánach – The Islandman.* The Blasket Centre in Dún Chaoin is dedi-cated to this unique literary output.

Music was also part of the islands; fiddles were made and played and many a song composed and sung. Inis Mhic Uibhleán is said to be haunted by the sweet other world sound of 'Port na bPúcaí'.

Ballybunion golf course *[photo: courtesy of Shannon Development]*

St John's, Listowel *[photo: courtesy of St John's Theatre and Arts Centre, Listowel]*

Siamsa Tíre, Tralee [photo: courtesy of Shannon Development]

Crag Caves [photo: courtesy of Shannon Development]

Blennerville Windmill [photo: courtesy of Shannon Development]

A ride on a jaunting car [photo: courtesy of Shannon Development]

Glanleam, Valentia island [photo: courtesy of Cork Kerry Tourism]

Skellig Michael [photo: courtesy of Cork Kerry Tourism]

Old Kenmare Road [photo: courtesy of Cork Kerry Tourism]

Slea Head and Blasket Islands *[photo: courtesy of Cork Kerry Tourism]*

Traditional fishing boat – the Curragh *[photo: courtesy of Cork Kerry Tourism]*

Ladies View, Killarney *[photo: courtesy of Cork Kerry Tourism]*

Muckross traditional farms *[photo: courtesy of Cork Kerry Tourism]*

Kerry Bog Ponies *[photo: courtesy of The Kerry Bog Village]*

Cill Rialaig, Ballinskelligs *[photo: courtesy of Noelle Campbell-Sharp]*

TOM CREAN
ANTARCTIC EXPLORER

From Annascaul to the Antarctic suggests a title for a true story – the story of Annascaul man Tom Crean, who was a hero of the British Antarctic Expedition in 1910 under the command of Captain Robert Falcon Scott, CVO, RN. Proof of Crean's valour, humour and fortitude on that expedition (he had served Captain Scott on a previous expedition in 1904) is contained both in the text and in the dedication of a thrilling book, *South With Scott,* written by one of Captain Scott's lieutenants, Admiral Sir R. G. R. Evans. The book recalls many incidents, which earned for Petty Officer Thomas Crean, RN, the respect and affection of all. The dedication reads: 'To Lashly and Crean this book is affectionately dedicated'.

On one occasion, Evans, Lashly and Crean found themselves in the heart of the Great Ice Fall halfway down the Beardmore Glacier. Only their superb physical condition allowed them to literally carry their sledge, weighing 400 pounds, for mile after mile. Eventually they arrived on a ridge between two stupendous open gulfs with only a narrow bridge of ice connecting them. Below was a seemingly bottomless chasm. Evans takes up the story: 'To cross by the connecting bridge was, to say the least of it, a precarious proceeding. After a minute's rest, we placed the sledge on this ice bridge and, as Crean described it afterwards – "We went along the crossbar into the H of Hell". Lashly, who went ahead, sat astride the bridge and was paid out at the end of the Alpine rope. He shuffled his way across fearful to look down into the icy blue chasm below.'

With his eyes fixed to the opposite wall of ice, Lashly got across and onto the top of the ice ridge. Crean and Evans now had to cross, with Lashly hauling carefully on the rope. The two sat astride the bridge of ice facing one another, balancing the sledge precariously between them. Neither of them spoke but stared into each other's eyes, not daring to look down. As they gazed at each other on that perilous icy crossing, little facial details remained with them forever.

Sadly for the expedition, the Norwegians led by Amundsen reached the South Pole before them. The Norwegian dogs proved more efficient than the British ponies for ice-trekking. Scott and some others met their deaths on the ice. Tom Crean survived and undaunted, subsequently served with Sir Ernest Shackleton's Trans-Antarctic expedition in 1914, when he took part in the epic open-boat journey to South Georgia. In 1996, a seven-man Irish expedition including Tralee man Mike Barry, retraced this journey in a boat named for Tom Crean, which they sadly lost. But they did traverse South Georgia where they erected a plaque in honour of all Irish Polar explorers.

Tom Crean from the South Pole Inn Annascaul was awarded the Royal Geographical Silver Medal and from the king, The Albert Medal for Bravery.

KILLORGLIN

Killorglin is, arguably, Kerry's friendliest town, certainly as to its location – not too far from anyplace in the county. There is easy access to Tralee to the north, Killarney to the east, through Castlemaine to west Kerry, and it is the gateway southward to where the warm heart of Kerry is all embracing. But, Killorglin has charm aplenty in its own right. Architecturally, it has retained many of the features typical of an early twentieth century Irish country town.

Converging roads from Tralee and Killarney merge at the bridge over the salmon-rich Laune River, and go straight up to the square at the top of the hill. The town square entertains King Puck on his high throne where he reigns at Lughnasa, August, each year to rule over the Puck Fair celebrations. This three-day fair is said by some to date back to pagan times, while others say the goats came charging into the town, warning of the advancing Cromwellian soldiers, and so, the goat is honoured ever since! Such is the royal perch of King Puck that, on his right, he can view the McGillicuddy Reeks in friendly silhouette while also giving royal acknowledgement to Carrantuohil, Ireland's highest mountain peak.

Killorglin points the way to Caragh Lake, Glenbeigh, Rossbeigh, and straight on to Iveragh through Kells and Mountain Stage. Masses of the beautiful purple and red fuchsia are everywhere; its glamour belying its Gaelic name, *Deora Dé* – God's Tears.

From the period 1893 to 1937, it was possible to take the train from Killorglin to Valentia Harbour. The line crossed two viaducts, through three tunnels and, on the six-mile stretch between Mountain Stage and Kells, the track sat on a narrow shelf just 270 feet above Dingle Bay, overlooking some of the most spectacular scenery in Europe.

Killorglin's beautifully designed railway station buildings, house, gardens and goods' store have been tastefully converted for use by private business and industry, a shining example of intelligent recycling! Thanks to the combined efforts of the Church of Ireland and Roman Catholic communities, the former now has a lovely church on the site.

KERRY WOOLLEN MILLS

Kerry Woollen Mills, Ballymalis, Beaufort, has a centuries old authority which, on a first viewing of the exterior, is concealed in a superficial time warp. Wonderful old stone buildings date back to the seventeenth century when King Charles II of England granted a charter to merchant Edward Sealy to establish a woollen manufacturing industry. It is ideally situated because of its easy access to Killorglin, Killarney and within nodding distance of the road to West Kerry.

Of prime importance to the mills is the proximity of the River Gweestin, a tributary of the Laune – itself the main outflow of the Killarney Lakes. Ever since the seventeenth century, the Gweestin has provided ideal soft water for washing and dyeing the raw wool. But, not alone was the quality of the water important, its power was also essential to drive the wooden water turbine. A steel unit replaced this turbine in 1928 and this still supplies fifty-horse power for the mill to this day.

A lane bordered with unspoilt lush hedgerows and old stone bridges leads into the yard of Kerry Woollen Mills around which a conglomerate of seemingly peaceful old buildings belies the hectic activity within. The wooden beamed shop interior is akin to an artist's palette with high fashion glowing and muted colours –

reds, greens, browns and a blue – blend straight from the nearby McGillicuddy Reeks.

Who chooses the colours and designs? The latest member of the Eadie family to take over the mills, Andrew. He is a graduate of the Scottish College of Textiles. His great-grandfather came from County Fermanagh in 1902 to buy the mill from the Sealy family. And Andrew's father Eric ran the business until his retirement in 1989. Andrew himself visits Paris for fashion updates and forecasts and employs a freelance designer as needs be.

The result of all this research and expertise is evidenced in the softest of sweaters, shawls, ruanas, stoles, scarves, rugs and blankets. The beautiful horse rugging is often bought for curtaining, while a rug in hot mustard with a red and a black stripe for a prized racehorse is enough to make any human envious!

With two retail outlets apart, there is also one in Adare, the mill fills local and national contracts with a large American mail order business. The mystery of the warp and the weft are explained on a tour of the mill. Kerry Woollen Mills was one of eight finalists in the 1996 Kerry Marketing Awards Competition.

SIGERSON CLIFFORD

Sigerson Clifford and Cahersiveen are synonymous. He grew up in the steep side street that climbs the hill behind the town – Barr na Sraide. Though born in Cork, he was brought to Cahersiveen while still a baby and, according to his wife Marie, 'he regarded himself as a loyal son of Kerry'.

> *I am Kerry like my mother before me*
> *And my mother's mother and her man.*
> *Now I sit on an office stool remembering*
> *And the memory of them like a fan*
> *Soothes the embers into flame*
> *I am Kerry and proud of my name*

The 'office stool' in the poem refers to his job with the Civil Service in Dublin. But, though Dublin based, Clifford wrote wonderful ballad poems, which capture with integrity and largely unsanitised nostalgia, his early memories of growing up in Cahersiveen. He was also an Abbey Theatre playwright – his best-known play, *Nano*, is still revived by amateur companies.

'The Boys of Barr na Sraide' is the essence of Clifford, capturing as it does his love of his people and of his country. But he will be remembered with great affection also for all his other stories in verse, written in simple uncomplicated metres, disdaining obscure symbolism.

In his poems of the Travelling People he projects a mix of subjective, non judgmental caring and clear objective observation; the ballads of a Tinker's Daughter, Tinker's Son, Tinker's Wife and the Tale of the Tinker Man. The tongue-in-cheek gentle sending-up of old times is delightfully illustrated in 'Gubby Donovan's Pig' and 'Lenihan's Big Bazaar'. The latter apart, all the others and more are included in *Ballads of a Bogman*, published in 1955 by Macmillan of London and recently reprinted by Mercier Press.

A quote from his very detailed funeral instructions tells of Sigerson Clifford's healthy cynicism of the human condition. 'Soon as the coffin arrives pop me in, screw down the lid and tell those who want to stare at me to shove off. When they didn't come to admire me when I was worth looking at, I don't want them peering at me when I can't see what they're thinking about me'. He is buried at Kilnavarnogue.

> *I'll take my sleep in those green fields the place my life began,*
> *Where the boys of Barr na Sraide went hunting for the wran.*

CAHERSIVEEN

*T'ainm on Dhia but there it is, the Dawn on the Hills of
Ireland. God's angels lifting the night's black veil from the fair
sweet face of my Ireland. Oh, Ireland isn't it grand, you look
like a bride in her rich adornin' – and with all the pent up love
of my heart, I bid you the top of the mornin'!*

So wrote John Locke as he echoed the sentiments of a
returning emigrant from the United States on his first
sighting of Ireland, while standing on the ship's side at
dawn. Locke's poem goes on: 'And Kerry is pushing her
headlands out to give us a kindly greeting!'

Kerry has three very large headlands or peninsulas
which reached out to many ships as they made their way
to Queenstown, now Cobh. Iveragh is the largest of these.
Corca Dhuibhne to the north and Beara to the south,
which we share with County Cork, comprise the other
two.

Cahersiveen is the capital town of the Iveragh Peninsula. It is perched on a rim of the Ferta River estuary and
at the base of Cahersiveen mountain. It would seem that
even before history was recorded, people settled here as
is endorsed by the fourth and fifth-century ring forts of
Cahergal and Leacanabuaile. Later, during Gaeldom's
last stand, the McCarthys built their finest castle on the
site of an O'Shea fortress. Like so much of Kerry, the land
was settled by the British government on Trinity College

Dublin. This did not stop Cahersiveen from mushrooming in the nineteenth century. It derives its name from yet another ring fort – Cathair Saidhbhin, Siveen's Fort.

The O'Connell family dominated the area for many years, managing to reconcile loyalties to Ireland, the British crown and to the French Republic. The most famous descendant, Daniel O'Connell, the Liberator, from Derrynane, has the town's fine granite Roman Catholic church named after him. A walk along Cahersiveen's long main street gives little indication of its close proximity to river and sea. The town's much-loved poet and balladeer, Sigerson Clifford, wrote:

> *Oh the town it climbs the mountain and looks upon the sea.*
> *And sleeping time or waking 'tis there I long to be,*
> *To walk again that kindly street, the place I grew a man,*
> *And the Boys of Barr na Sraide went hunting for the wran.*

The Fenian Cycle, the Fianniacht, includes many legends of Fionn MacCumhaill and the Fianna in the Cahersiveen area. In one of these stories, so effective was Fionn in frightening a giant who had come in from the sea, that the giant high-tailed it off back to the sea in such a hurry that he stepped on Valentia Island on the way and, in so doing, formed another island, Beginish!

Tá trí leabaí [three beds] *Diarmuid agus Gráinne* in Iveragh. Diarmuid and Gráinne, the famous lovers of the Fianna, have three beds no less named after them – one in Filemore and two in Kells.

On a more practical level, Valentia Observatory began on the island in 1860 and based in Cahersiveen is known through the western world for its weather reports. The restored RIC barracks holds evidence of the areas heritage, as well as housing a tourist facility and Radio Kerry's studio.

VALENTIA

Valentia's old-world atmosphere is bathed in nostalgia. There is an unchallenging restfulness, an over-riding feeling of the past being ever present. And, there is so much to remember!

Before the extraordinary Anglicisation of its name, Valentia was known as Oileán Dairbhre (Island of the Oaks). Oak trees are not so visible now but were plentiful when St Brendan made his regular visits in the fifth century. There is a holy well, Tobar Olla, named after him.

Visiting botanists have a rare time here, as do geologists and archaeologists. Recently discovered tracks on local slate of a Devonian Tetrapod, an early amphibious creature, has sent the geologists of Europe chasing back over 350 million years. There is also evidence of human occupation, which goes back over 6,000 years.

Of course, Valentia is no bleak, craggy island way out from the Iveragh coast in south-west Kerry. On the contrary, it has a lush sub-tropical air about it, warmed as it is by the waters of the Gulf Stream. To quote local historian, John O'Sullivan, 'it's lying cosily alongside the coast, not protruding out into the Atlantic as some people think'.

Because of the political influence of one-time resident landlord, the Knight of Kerry, who was one of the

Fitzgerald clan, Valentia prospered in the nineteenth century. The Slate Quarry was developed and Valentia slate was shipped to England in huge quantities and may be seen to this day in the walls of London's National Gallery and the House of Commons, among other public buildings. Now a Marian Grotto set deep in the quarry attracts both the devout and the curious, serving somehow to increase the rather lonely air of a once busy centre of industry.

By contrast, Glanleam House and gardens, once home to the Knight of Kerry, welcomes the visitor in magnificent style. Described as 'Europe's most Westerly', Glanleam's sub-tropical gardens offer unique exotica. A safari-like feel accompanies the walker through authentic tropical jungle, emerging to panoramic views of land and sea and, delightfully, a cup of tea!

Valentia weather forecasts have long had European recognition. The first telegraph weather report was sent to London in 1862 and, in 1867, Valentia Observatory was set up. In 1892, it transferred both itself and its name to Cahersiveen; so, Valentia and weather forecasting remain synonymous. Over the years, people of genius such as Morse, Bright, Field and Kelvin were attracted to the island. It was thanks to their combined efforts that the first Atlantic telegraph cable was laid between Valentia and Newfoundland in 1866.

A visit to the Heritage Centre whets the imagination for more stories of lighthouse and lifeboat men, of visiting pirates, Cromwellian soldiers and more. Famous Kerry footballer Mick O'Connell may be glimpsed either on land or sea. The shuttle car ferry to Knightstown begins an island ring, which ends over the bridge at Portmagee.

The Skelligs

Skellig Michael, Sceilig Mhichíl, and Small Skellig are two stark, beautiful, isolated crags of old red sandstone, rising like volcanoes out of the Atlantic Ocean, eight miles south-west of Valentia Island.

Under the ocean, which is warmed by the Gulf Stream from the Caribbean, the cliffs continue downwards to merge into the Continental Shelf. The story of the Skelligs is well illustrated in the Heritage Centre on Valentia Island. For example, the history and archaeology of Skellig Michael's early Christian monastery, and the fascinating world-wide travels of the hundreds and thousands of seabirds who make it their annual habitat are well documented. Breathtaking in summer is the sight of Europe's largest gannet colonies clinging to the cliffs. Memorabilia of the lighthouses that gave 161 years of service to mariners from many lands plays up the human factor of maritime history. And the fascinating peep into the life, colour and magic of underwater Skellig is a visual delight.

History leaning back into mythology surrounds the islands and records refer to a shipwreck nearly 3,400 years ago – even the King of the World is reputed to have visited the Skelligs in 200 AD!

In the sixth century a group of holy men set up a monastery in Skellig Michael, which is regarded as being among the finest and best preserved in the world. The beehive shaped stone cells make for unique monastic architecture, the signature of which is the corbelling technique of dry stone building. Two boat-shaped oratories, also terraces, walls and stairways, all built of stone, give witness to much early Christian activity. Five hand-cut water storage wells still function and are said to go dry only in cases of cursing, swearing or blasphemy! One of two St Finians is credited with founding this self-contained monastic wonder.

In the sixth century, the high seas were the highways and crossroads of the world; news travelled quickly, even to isolated islands like the Skelligs – a battle in Rome, an earthquake in Gaul, or a plundering in Iona.

Fashion came to Valentia from Southern Europe and North Africa – and Spanish wine brought cheer to many.

The monks left Sceilig in the eleventh century to join the Augustinian House in Ballinskelligs.

STAIGUE FORT

Stone forts are numerous on the west coast of Ireland, and Staigue Fort in south Kerry's beautiful Iveragh Peninsula is in a quite good state of preservation. Experts differ widely on dates and usage. Construction began maybe as early as 500 AD. Situated north of Castlecove; its sister fort, Cahergal, now in ruins, is but a short distance away near Cahersiveen, the capital town of Iveragh. The skill evident in the building of Staigue Fort is still a source of wonder today. No mortar was used and the stones were not dressed. The facing stones inside and outside were filled with spalls. The space between the inside and outside walls was filled with rubble. The wall has a striking curve and characteristics of the construction were to influence Irish building for centuries to come.

An unusual feature of the interior, not much of which remains intact, were the ten X-shaped double staircases. Were the fort to be used as an amphitheatre, then as a form of seating, these stairs provided excellent viewing. Another theory put forward suggests that in time of attack the stairs were used to dash to the top of the fort and take on the enemy. Or maybe they were just decorative – who knows? Two small doorways lead into two cells, each seven feet high. They may have been used to store food or to jail wrongdoers, as either occasion arose.

Since there exists no tangible proof of the builder's

intentions, perhaps the original purpose of Staigue Fort is best left to the imagination, as indeed is the identity of those early builders. They were miners some say, who came to excavate the copper in the area. Another story tells of thirty boats with thirty people in each boat arriving from North Africa and proceeding to build stone forts all over the area. Some say the fairies, the little people, built them! Legends abound.

According to writer Sigerson Clifford, some antiquarian dug up a skull in nearby Cahergal Fort. The skull had a pipe between his or her teeth – proof, if it were needed, that Kerry people were smoking long before the Spaniards brought tobacco to Iveragh!

Daniel O'Connell

'The Irish are not sufficiently enlightened to bear the sun of freedom'. These words were spoken by Daniel O'Connell – famous Kerryman, sophisticated European and brilliant lawyer – when he decided *not* to support Thomas Davis and the other Young Irelanders. O'Connell did not believe in bloodshed, not even to obtain freedom. While studying in France he witnessed some of the excesses of the French Revolution and was to become very suspicious of what are now sometimes termed 'freedom fighters'.

Daniel's uncle, Daniel Charles O'Connell, served in France all through the French Revolution and was to be the last general of the Irish Brigade. He was awarded the Order of St Louis, the sash of which was always kept at Lakeview, Killarney, while the star remained at the home of direct O'Connell descendants, the McCarthy O'Leary family, Coomlagane, Millstreet. This is now home to the Equestrian Centre at Green Glens. When Elizabeth McCarthy O'Leary married Sir Morgan O'Connell of Lakeview, her aunt gave the star to her husband as a wedding present, reuniting both sash and star in Killarney.

It was one of Daniel's brothers, James, who built Lakeview in 1870 on obtaining a baronetcy for political services. Sir Maurice O'Connell, son of Lady Elizabeth and the late Sir Morgan, now lives there.

Daniel O'Connell was born in August 1775 at Car-hen House, Cahersiveen, to Morgan O'Connell – who ran a flourishing salt industry – and Catherine Mullane. Catherine, mother of Daniel, is remembered by the family to this day for bringing cocked noses into the family!

It was to the Iveragh Peninsula that O'Connell owed his early influences. His uncle, Maurice Huntingcap O'Connell was so called because, refusing to pay the government hat tax, he always wore a hunting cap. Maurice, having no children, made Daniel his heir to Derrynane House. A clever boy, Daniel, after early school-ing in Cobh, went to study in France and later to Lin-coln's Inn, London. Because he was a Catholic, he was denied entry to Ireland's only university, Trinity College. He was called to the Irish Bar in 1798 and pursued a bril-liant career.

Daniel O'Connell was propelled into politics on see-ing the British renege on their promises after the passing of the Act of Union in 1800. Having won Catholic Eman-cipation in 1829, he embarked on a campaign to repeal the Act of Union, was elected MP for County Clare, ar-rested, tried as a traitor and imprisoned for three months in Richmond Jail. Broken in health and spirit, he went to the continent to recover, but died in Genoa in 1847. His heart was taken to Rome and his body to Glasnevin in Dublin, where a round tower was erected to his memory in 1869.

CASTLECOVE AND AN ENGLISH REBEL

Lady Albinia Lucy Broderick of Castlecove was by no means the first Briton to see Ireland as fertile soil on which to plant philanthropic zeal. Nor was she the first to shed her Anglo image by becoming fluent in Irish, even translating her name to Gobnait Ní Bhruadair. Micheál Mac Liammóir did it in the performing arts and, together with his partner who was also English, Hilton Edwards, established Dublin's Gate Theatre as an international playhouse. Patrick Pearse, son of an Englishman, became Pádraig Mac Piarais and spearheaded the 1916 Easter Revolution.

Lady Albinia was unusual in that she was the daughter of an English landlord, William Freemantle Broderick, Viscount Midleton and Mary Broderick neé Freemantle. Albinia was born at Chester Square, Middlesex (Belgravia) in 1861. Education given by private tutors, all probably English, was to leave her with an extraordinary idealism. This, together with matching energy, was to benefit the Castlecove area of south Kerry.

A beautiful coastal area, it saw bloody battles in the seventeenth century between nearby occupying British garrisons and the local parishes in the Ballinskelligs, Castlecove and Westcove areas. Following the defeat of a garrison in 1644, the British government ordered the natives to leave the whole peninsula south of the river Laune and west of the river Finnihy, on penalty of death.

It was into this depressed area that Albinia Broderick came in the twentieth century to attempt to redress some of her fellow-Britons' wrongs. And she was well suited to such a mission having developed her talents on many fronts. She managed her uncle's household in Oxford; he was Warden of Merton College. She also wrote on matters scientific for the newspapers; published a book of poetry; qualified as a nurse in Dublin and became proficient in the Irish language.

It was while visiting the family estates in Midleton that Albinia witnessed the evils of landlordism. Turning her back on her British imperial background, she bought sixteen acres of land at Westcove and built an agricultural co-operative and a hospital. The co-op remained open until 1945. The hospital failed to attract doctors, probably because of its remoteness. According to Pádraig Ó Loinsigh's biography, *as Gaeilge,* the hospital's only patient was a priest who fell off his bicycle. Albinia, or Gobnait, became active in the War of Independence and warned Michael Collins against the Treaty: 'I know what I'm talking about. I lived with British diplomats and worked in the War Office'. Lady Albinia Broderick or Gobnait Ní Bhruadair died in 1955 and is buried in Sneem. The remains of her buildings can still be seen near Castlecove.

Sneem

Sneem, widely acknowledged as the loveliest village of
the south-west, carries its image with style and grace.
The town is an oft-times winner of the national Tidy
Towns competition. It is hard to believe now that about
250 years ago, although Sneem was not greatly affected
by the Great Famine, it was described by a visitor as a
'poor, dirty village'.

Now, into a new millennium, it welcomes national
and international dignitaries with unaffected sophisti-
cation. Indeed some unable to cast off its spell, quite
simply stayed! Famous guests of happy memory include
the late Princess Grace of Monaco; the Queen of the Net-
herlands; General Charles de Gaulle of France. A vivid
reminder of the latter's visit can be seen in the North
Square where an impressive boulder of local stone,
sculpted by Alan Hall, carries a De Gaulle medallion
which bears an inscribed quote from the general: *En ce
moment de ma longue vie, j'ai trouvé ici ce que je cherchais:
être en face de moi-même. L'Irlande me offert de la façon la plus
delicate, la plus amicale.* ('At this grave moment of my long
life, I found here what I sought, to be face to face with
myself. Ireland gave me that, in the most delicate, the
friendliest way'.) A bouquet indeed!

No less than three memorial sculptures commemor-
ate a former President of Ireland, Cearbhaill Ó Dálaigh,

who, with his wife Máirín, retired to Sneem. He died there and was given a state funeral to the local cemetery.

Cearbhaill Ó Dálaigh, a brilliant lawyer, immersed himself in many diverse cultures with extraordinary effect. An inspiring stainless steel friendship tree, carrying inscriptions in Hebrew, Irish and English followed a Vivienne Roche sculpture in the South Square. President Chaim Herzog of Israel, an Irishman presented this tree, in 1985. And, not to be outdone, in 1986, in recognition of Cearbhaill Ó Dálaigh's work for China's admission into the United Nations, the People's Republic of China donated a white marble panda; it sits peacefully on a rock in a small bamboo garden at the entrance to the Pier Road. An inscription expresses the admirable wish that 'the friendship between the peoples of China and Ireland live forever'.

It is of little wonder that Sneem's international sculpture collection has won widespread admiration and recognition. Wonderful contrasts carry through, from Joseph McNally's 'Risen Christ' on the grounds of the Roman Catholic church to James Scanlon's nearby fascinating landscape trail 'The Way the Fairies Went'. Across the way, Isis, Goddess of Protection, a gift from the people of Egypt, seems to gaze caringly across as the fairies and humans wend their way. Colourful streetscapes and subtropical vegetation adds to a certain quirkiness in Sneem's presentation of itself and is very attractive. It boasts two squares no less – the North Square, which is really the west, and the South Square, which is the east! A narrow bridge over the River Sneem joins the two squares, each of which is really a triangle!

A narrow pedestrian way parallel to the bridge boasts an illusory exit, while the Church of Ireland's weather vane sports a salmon instead of a cock.

The name Sneem comes from the Irish *Sniadhm* meaning 'A Knot'. And what does the knot signify? There are as many answers to that ever-present question as there is colour and character in Sneem.

FATHER O'FLYNN

Of priests we can offer a charmin' variety,
Far renowned for larnin' and piety;
Still, I'd advance you without impropriety,
Father O'Flynn as the flower of them all.
Here's a health to you, Father O'Flynn,
Sláinte, and sláinte, and sláinte agin.
Powerfullest preacher, and
Tinderset teacher, and
Kindliest creature in auld Donegal!

'The Ballad of Father O'Flynn' was written by Alfred Percival Graves of Parknasilla and based on Father Michael Walsh – or 'Father Mihil' or perhaps 'Father Michíl'. Father Walsh was a colourful parish priest of Sneem during the middle of the nineteenth century. The last line of the chorus is puzzling in that Graves uses 'Donegal' instead of a local place name. It is thought that this happened for reasons of rhyme and rhythm.

It would appear Father Walsh was a very sporting and gregarious individual whose love of the field sports fitted the image of a Protestant parson rather than a Catholic priest, a reason perhaps for his friendship with Dean Charles Graves, the Anglican rector. Dean Graves, together with his wife and family, leased part of what was later to become the Parknasilla Hotel. The two clerics also shared a great love of the Irish language, and Father Walsh was also an accomplished violinist. By the time

Dean Graves was appointed Bishop of Limerick in 1866, firm links of friendship had been forged between the Graves family and Father Walsh:

> *Don't talk of your Provost and Fellows of Trinity,*
> *Famous forever at Greek and Latinity*
> *Bad and the divils and all at Divinity*
> *Father O'Flynn'd make hares of them all.*
> *Come, I venture to give you my word,*
> *Never the like of his logic was heard*
> *Down from mythology, into theyology*
> *Troth, and conchology, if he'd the call.*

This unusual priest obviously left an indelible impression on young Alfred Graves. Having graduated from Trinity College in 1871, he went to work in London in the Home Office. While walking to work one morning, suddenly finding himself whistling an Irish traditional tune, 'The Top of the Cork Road', images of Father O'Flynn – or 'Father Mihil' – flashed through his mind and 'The Ballad of Father O'Flynn' was written in his head before he reached the office:

> *Och, Father O'Flynn, you've a wonderful way wid you*
> *All ould sinners are wishful to pray wid you*
> *All the young childer are wild for to play wid you*
> *You've such a way wid you, Father avick,*
> *Still, for all you've so gentle a soul,*
> *Gad, you've your flock in the grandest control*
> *Checking the crazy ones,*
> *Coaxin' on aisy ones*
> *Liftin the lazy ones on wid the stick.*

And though quite avoidin' all foolish frivolity
Still at all seasons of innocent jollity
Where was the playboy could claim an equality
At comicality, Father, wid you?
Once the Bishop looked grave at your jest,
Till this remark set him off wid the rest
'Is it lave gaity
all to the laity?
Cannot the clargy be Irishmen too?'

The chorus is of course interspersed between the verses
and rounds it all off:

So, here's a health to you, Father O'Flynn
Sláinte and sláinte, and sláinte agin
Powerfullest preacher, and
Tinderest teacher, and
Kindliest creature in auld Donegal!

Father Walsh, parish priest of Sneem, died in 1866, never
to know that he would be remembered by an affection-
ate stage-Irish ballad written in London by the son of
Dean Graves, his old friend of the cloth, albeit a cloth of
a different cut!

TUOSIST

Standing proudly at the gateway to the Beara Peninsula, Tuosist beckons the visitor through, into a magical strip of Kerry, 20 miles long at the edge of the Kenmare Bay. The Beara Peninsula dips its headlands into the Atlantic Ocean where it is warmed by the Gulf Stream, resulting in exotic sub-tropical plant and shrub growth.

Counties Kerry and Cork share this wonderland. The Miskish and Caha mountains form the spine, which divides these oft-times sporting rivals. The rivalry on the football field between these two Beara tribes was illustrated by one of Tuosist's many poets, 'Murty Larry', as long ago as the end of the nineteenth century.

'There was a football game between the Bearaghs and the Kerrymen. It would cheer the heart of anyone to see the gallant play.' The poet goes on at great length and with great glee to celebrate in verse the Kerrymen's victory over the Castletownbere men. Sporting prowess apart, since the beginning of the 1960s, Tuosist can boast a regrowth and a renewal that reflects an unusual, indeed an almost unique, sense of place and self.

Luckily, there was a guiding light in the person of the parish priest, Fr John Scanlon. Fr Scanlon was galvanised into action on discovering in the early 1960s that the last child had been enrolled in one of the parish schools and there was no prospect of another for the near future.

Emigration and unemployment had taken their toll; state agencies did not want to know. A similar situation existed all along the western seaboard. It was then that Fr Scanlon heard of the Legion of Mary's work in promoting farmhouse holidays in Inchigeela in Co. Cork.

With huge dedication and energy, the community and Frank Duff's Legion were brought together. The parish of Tuosist, with its three components Dauros, Cloonee and Lauragh, was revitalised and opened a farmhouse to tourists on a wet St Patrick's weekend in 1963. But our patron saint smiled on Tuosist through the rain. And now, in the new Millennium, cross community involvement has created a new parish dynamic and a vibrant tourist industry. Pride in the past has evoked new interest in local history, heritage and folklore; centuries old poetry has been rediscovered and the poets honoured.

Éigse Sheáin Uí Shúilleabháin has been established to celebrate Tuosist's most famous son, eminent folklorist Dr Seán Ó Súilleabháin. Sporting lass and international athlete, runner Maureen Harrington, races upwards and onwards.

A ring of Beara trail brings Kerry and Cork together in celebration of the peninsula's beauty and history, while the ages-old stone circles of Tuosist reflect a timeless sun, rising, setting and always rising again.

KENMARE

Kenmare, described as 'the jewel on the Ring of Kerry', looks out over Kenmare Bay – *Inver Scéine*, the bay's old name *as Gaeilge*. Judging by its popular use, the town's name *as Gaeilge* – *Neidín* – has more appeal for song-writers and storytellers than its anglicised version. This is perhaps because *Neidín* translates into 'little nest', an apt description of the town's cosy situation, nestling as it does between the Rings of Kerry and Beara with the mountains for protection.

Proof of the Gulf Stream's influence is the luxuriant sub-tropical growth of which there is much glorious evidence.

Kenmare has been designated a Bord Fáilte Heritage Town under the theme of 'A Planned Estate Town'. This is hardly surprising since surveyor John Powell at the instruction of William Petty Fitzmaurice II – Earl of Shelbourne – carefully planned the town in the early eighteenth century. The same William Petty Fitzmaurice was to become Prime Minister of Britain in 1782.

In more recent times, another Prime Minister of Britain, Margaret Thatcher, came to visit. The history of the Petty family's connection with Kenmare goes back to the early seventeenth century. It began with an all-round genius, William Petty, who had many accomplishments: a reformer in the fields of taxation and politics; a professor of music and a physician. It was in this latter capacity that he came to Ireland as Physician General to Cromwell's forces. He was knighted and given huge tracts of land in the Kenmare area – ousting at least one Irish chieftain, O'Sullivan Beare, from his lands at Tuosist.

But happily for Kenmare as it stands today, the influence of that first William Petty extended down the generations to William Petty Fitzmaurice II, and to some inspired town-planning.

Kenmare has had artistic influences going back through a couple of centuries; Thackeray and Tennyson came to visit, E. J. Moeran composed some of his music there while Thomas Moore regaled many a drawing-room gathering with his melodies. Kenmare Lace is famous the world over, thanks to a congregation of Poor Clare nuns. Another nun, Margaret Cusack, was to become known as a pioneering feminist and a revolutionary thinker.

MICHAEL LEHANE
MORLEY'S BRIDGE HERO

Michael Lehane, Spanish soldier, Norwegian seaman, native of Morley's Bridge near Kilgarvan in the Roughty Valley, was a hero of two wars. Thwarted from buying a farm through lack of funds, having taken an agricultural course in Clonakilty College, Lehane went to Dublin where he worked as a builder's labourer and joined the United Builders Labourers' Trade Union. Like several other young Irish idealists, a foreign cause beckoned him. In December 1936, aged twenty-eight years, he went to Spain to enlist in Frank Ryan's Irish unit of the International Brigades, to defend the Spanish Republic against both domestic fascist revolt and foreign fascist invasion. Michael Lehane was one of a hundred-and-forty-five Irishmen who enlisted in the International Brigades – sixty-one were killed in action. A few still survive to tell many a heroic tale.

Lehane enlisted in December and on Christmas Eve was fighting on the Cordoba Front, where nine of the Irish unit were killed in action. The following month saw him defending the Spanish capital in the Battle of Las Rossas de Madrid. Returning from a few months' home leave, he rejoined his unit to take part in July's Battle of Brunete where his heroism, while rescuing wounded comrades, is legendary. Severely wounded himself, the hero from Morley's Bridge came home to recuperate and returned via the Pyrenees to Catalunya to join the poorly armed Spanish Republicans for the final offensive, leading to victory for the fascist forces of Franco. Four of his best friends died in the Battle of Gandesa – Londoner Max Nash, O'Sullivan from Dublin, Derryman George Gorman and Jim Straney of Belfast. A wounded Lehane escaped with the help of Michael O'Riordan. On a sunny Sunday in the summer of 1985, the Last Post sounded over Morley's Bridge as a large crowd stood to attention and then listened in rapt silence while Michael O'Riordan told of Michael Lehane's heroic deeds in the fight for the Republican cause in Spain.

But Michael Lehane's idealistic commitment to his fellowman did not end in Spain. From the building sites of Birmingham, he heard of the rantings of Adolf Hitler in Germany. Hitler had to be stopped! To wear a British army uniform was anathema to Lehane. He signed on as fireman/stoker with the Norwegian navy. His charmed life ran out in March 1943 when his ship was torpedoed by a Nazi submarine. Norwegian attention was drawn to the Irish hero through an article written by Manus O'Riordan, Michael's son, in 1995. As soon as the article was brought to their notice, the Norwegian authorities took immediate action. In 1996, Michael Lehane's brother Stephen was located in Birmingham and the Norwegian Ministry of Foreign Affairs awarded him the Norwegian War Medal in memory of his brother Michael's noble record in the cause of humanity.

No paseran! They will not pass! This was the Republican slogan in the Spanish Civil War. The memory of Michael Lehane from Morley's Bridge in the beautiful valley of the Roughty will certainly not pass!

THE ROUGHTY RIVER
VALLEY AND KILGARVAN

The Roughty River rises in the Cork / Kerry border and, on its way to join the sea at Kenmare Bay, this colourful river creates its own independent barony. Glenrought, encompasses the three southernmost Kerry parishes, Kenmare, Tuosist and Kilgarvan. Two main tributaries reinforce the Roughty, the Owbeg to the north over which towers magnificent Mangerton, while from the south, the Slaheny is greeted on arrival by the capital of the Roughty Valley – Kilgarvan.

Kilgarvan epitomises the colour and independence of the Roughty River and Valley. A Republic of Kilgarvan perhaps? Perhaps! An article by Tomás Ó Murchadha humorously assesses the idea in an impeccably researched book *Kilgarvan in the Beautiful Valley of the Roughty,* edited by Frank Shanley and Mary Kelliher. Ó Murchadha suggests that Kilgarvan is self-contained, being bordered by mountains to the north and south. All that is needed is to blow up four bridges and there you have it – a republic. Just raise the flag! Ó Murchadha lists off four home-grown heroes of the new republic – in the style of Homer, Shakespeare, Swift and Marx. The Marx think-alike is presumably Mick Quill, the famous American Labour leader who was born in Kilgarvan in 1905.

The fact that the McCarthys kept Kilgarvan and the valley of the Roughty and, indeed, the entire south-west free from invasion for 300 years in the thirteenth century, tells not alone of their power but also of the defensibility of the area. In that century, the then chief devised a brilliant manoeuvre to defeat a thousand-strong Norman force at the Battle of Callan. Sadly, Dónal an Cárthach Finín was killed in the battle. His name is still honoured in the Roughty Valley six hundred years later.

From the end of the eighteenth century to the late 1980s about eight acres along the banks of the Roughty hosted annually what was surely a unique mix of racing, all in one day. Hares, greyhounds, donkeys, and even motorcycles tested their skills. People attended in droves from Kenmare, Bantry, Macroom and even Dingle. This valley's story is endless and seamless. Politicians, poets, soldiers, folklorists and sporting heroes weave in and out of it. To famous son Jackie Healy Rae goes the last word. In reply to Madge Hegarty's question 'Is there life after death?': 'I don't know but, I'll tell you one thing, I will live out life until the last minute and let the last hour be the toughest. One thing is for certain, considering all the hours I have put in over the past few years, I will have lived at least twice as long as a lot of people!'

SLIABH LUACHRA
A PLACE APART

Mix an Indian goddess with a dispossessed people living on a rushy mountain and you might begin to solve the riddle of Sliabh Luachra. The first recorded people to live here on the east Kerry/west Cork border were evicted from their lands in Laois/Offaly during the Elizabethan Plantations of 1558. Refugees fleeing from the Munster Plantations of 1585 came to join them. So rough was the area that a report sent to Elizabeth I declared the terrain to be 'impassable'. It was not so apparently for the mere native Irish.

Danu, the Indian goddess of fertility, whose breasts – *dha cioch Dana* or 'The Paps' – feature as mountains presiding over the Sliabh Luachra landscape, might provide the key to the area's wealth of music and poetry. She is said to have given her name to two rivers, the Danube and the Danau, as she traversed Europe before finally forming a backdrop for Sliabh Luachra, at Rathmore, where she continues to rest her magnificent mountainous breasts full of fertile promise. A cairn on each breast forms her nipples. When one considers the oft-suggested link between Indian and Irish sean nós singing – then perhaps? Who knows?

Of course, another story suggests that she was Dana,

Goddess of the Tuatha de Danann. The fact is that east of Killarney, between the Abha na Croí river and the Munster Blackwater, the landscape is dotted with unsolved riddles. Near Gneeveguille, a Gullane or Standing Stone in a field is visible from the road. There is no available explanation as to why it was put there over 4,000 years ago. There were twelve such stones standing in a line between there and Lisigiveen in Killarney, probably concealing some prehistoric pagan mystery. Like concentric Celtic circles, the mix of cryptic prehistoric stones and a huge fertility symbol gazing down on a rushy mountainous land has produced an indomitable human force out of which emerged Sliabh Luachra's unique contribution to Irish literature and music.

Defining Sliabh Luachra in musical terms is a subject of many debates. Journalist and native son Con Houlihan says ''Tis consuming up the whole country'. Ciarán Mac Mathúna suggests that 'when the Irish language died in this part of the country, the tradition lived on in the music'. Thankfully, it did not happen before Rathmore Jesuit priest P. S. Dineen produced his famous dictionary.

Traditional players began to be recognised in America in the 1900s. At home, RTÉ, through Seamus Ennis, recorded Glenntain's fiddle-master Pádraig O'Keefe in the 1940s. Many well-known pupils carry on the tradition. Sadly, Julia Clifford died in 1996 in England. Another player, Johnny Leary, is a famous accordion player and the singers are everywhere – like Christy Cronin and 'the charming Quarry Cross'. Actor and *seanachaí* Eamon Kelly expresses his own unique talent.

Compliments of Cumann Luachra two native poets are remembered in stone: Aogán Ó Rathaille and Owen Rua Ó Súilleabháin. A quote from an Ó Rathaille poem is inscribed on his memorial: *Aisling géar do dhearcas féin im' leaba is mé lag bríoch.* Owen Rua who died in 1784 aged 36, is also remembered from his own poetry: *'Ag taisteal na sléibhte dom seoladh im' aonar.'*

'And you'd need a tune in your heart', says Fr Pat Moore, to keep you going over the long narrow roads of the Sliabh Luachra mountains.

THE NIGHT THE BOG MOVED

Since the end of the seventeenth century, many bog slides have been recorded in Ireland but none had the tragic consequences of the Sliabh Luachra disaster during the Christmas period of 1896. Eight people died – all from the one family, when a water-soaked peaty mass heaved and moved through the night like a malign monster, covering acres of farmland and sweeping away an entire house and its inmates.

There was a calf fair in Killarney that day and John Riordan of Anneghbeg was preparing to make an early departure. Imagine his amazement and fright at the sight of a moving mountain of fire coming towards him at speed, making a noise like thunder. Hypnotised by the awesomeness of it all, his eyes followed the light until it disappeared near Barraduff. Apparently, the light was a powerful phosphorescent glow caused by underground chemical disturbances. The retching and movement continued throughout the next day accompanied by a noise like the booming of big guns. During all this time the tragedy of a missing family had to be faced up to. The Donnelly home, had quite simply disappeared, along with the father, mother and six of their seven children. Katie aged fifteen, had gone to visit her uncle – it was Christmas holiday time.

A Christmas candle in the window was the last sign of life anyone had witnessed of the Donnelly household. It was just a normal family. Some of the children, Daniel, Hannah, Humphrey, Margaret, James and Lizzie, aged between sixteen years and eighteen months, had probably played their own Sliabh Luachra music on that last night of their lives.

The parents were young also; Con Donnelly who was steward of the local limestone quarry, was only 44 and his wife, Johanna, was 38. The 1996 *Journal of Sliabh Luachra* outlines the events, one hundred years later. Con Casey describes the isolation and darkness of the night in the depths of winter. 'It was dark, dark, impenetrably dark, in the wetness of the mist and silence, silent as the tomb, at two o'clock in the morning of Monday 28 December 1896 in that mile-wide convex cover of swollen, heathery ground, then known as Beach na Meena, between the two roads that forked out from the Quarry Cross.'

In the same *Journal*, Donal Hickey outlines in graphic detail the reactions of neighbours, press and both local and central government. *The Kerry Sentinel* of 2 January noted: 'The only cheering sight was the earnestness and spontaneousness shown by the surrounding peasantry in searching for the bodies'. The bodies of Lizzie, James and Margaret were never found. Katie, the sole survivor, returned years later and built a house near the site of her old home. Cumann Luachra marked the tragic spot with a plaque.

Relief for the stricken people and support for Katie varied. Fr O'Sullivan, parish priest of Rathmore, and Lord Kenmare led the way. Local and central government were rather pathetic. Queen Victoria had the incident investigated and sent £5. Robert Lloyd Praeger, a member of the investigating committee, describes the scene in his book, *The Way That I Went:* 'It was dark, cold weather, the Reeks were white with snow – I well remember the feeling of depression with which we gazed at that black slimy mass stretching down the valley. Other bogs have burst but none so devastating as Knocknageeha'.

KILLARNEY

Although Dublin was long recognised as one of Europe's foremost cultural capitals, and welcomed many illustrious visitors over the centuries, only a small number of adventurous souls ventured into the south-west until the nineteenth century. Tales of Killarney's extraordinary beauty spread abroad, especially to Britain following a royal visit. It was in Britain that Thomas Cook set up the first ever travel agency in the 1850s. Railways with power-steamed locomotives began to criss-cross England and Ireland followed suit. Steam replaced sails to drive ships and travel became an accepted fact. The Bianconi horse-drawn cars provided regular services throughout Ireland, bringing about the development of many country inns.

In the mid-nineteenth century, the Bianconi Cork–Killarney trip took seven hours. On 16 July 1853, the Lord Lieutenant Lord Carlisle, officially opened the new railway line to Killarney. The express rail time from Dublin to Killarney took eight hours. A Railway Hotel was built, another hotel followed in the town. Killarney's – and indeed Kerry's – tourism took off.

Two worlds came to exist side by side. Only very rarely did one impinge on the other. The real world of Kerry's rural population was poor and beset by the nineteenth century land problems. The world created for the tourist developed into a sort of romantic fairyland. Travel-writers and commercial interests and that colourful pheno-menon, the tourist guide, combined to create a sort of spider parlour web into which tourists were lured – al-beit willingly, unlike the fly of the nursery rhyme. Kil-larney and its environs quickly became the mecca for tourism. Travellers took wonderful tales away with them. Fantasy, folktales, pagan and Christian rituals and events from the Fenian cycle featuring Fionn, Oisin, Niamh and the rest were woven into fantastic and entertaining stories.

Killarney's jarveys and boatmen became tourist at-tractions in themselves. In his book *Echo after Echo*, Donal Horgan tells of a jarvey explaining rainbows while driv-ing a party round the Muckross estate in his jaunting car: 'You'll have the greatest luck my lady – it isn't everyone that sees the Rainbow's Rest. There's them that would give all they have in the world – be it much or little – to see the foot of the rainbow. It's well known that there's a goldmine somewhere close. Sure, King Solomon in all his glory couldn't make the likes of it! And see how it's fading. It's as gone now, my lady, as if it had never been. You'll be in luck to have seen it.'

THE KERRY COW

The Kerry Cow is coming into its own again. This is thanks largely to the interest taken by the management of Muckross House and Killarney's National Park, coupled with the founding of the Rare Breed Society by Dr Leo Curran of University College Dublin under the auspices of the Royal Dublin Society. Dan Kelliher, Superintendent of the National Park, describes the Kerry Cow as 'a cow for the house'. In 1989, a poetic journalist saw her as 'a dainty Kerry Brunette' while commenting on the fact that five of the lovely creatures had been transferred from Muckross to Glenveigh National Park in Donegal. This forced exit was carried out apparently without benefit of a bull – whose love had to be sent hereafter by An Post. The practicality of the Kerry breed, as well as their beauty no doubt, was acknowledged all along the western seaboard ever since their arrival with the Celts thousands of years ago. They grazed happily at high altitudes and on the low foothills. They were 'hardy' – they still are. And in Europe, they continue to prove the point to this day in the mid altitudes of the Alps.

In Kerry, they now graze happily at the foot of the McGillicuddy Reeks and in the lawns and fields around Muckross House and Muckross Abbey. My late father would have been diverted at this upsurge of interest in the Kerry Cow. He loved his Kerry Cow and always kept one to supply the milk needs of the house while his family was growing up. And he was no farmer, but a station-master who was lucky enough to have two fields attached to his living in Killorglin. He always milked this precious cow himself; one of the railway porters milked the other resident bovines on whom my father hadn't really much *meas* but was hard-headed enough to boost the family income by selling their milk. Milking the 'black beauty' as he called his favourite had a great deal of ceremony attached. Two milking buckets were scalded with boiling water a couple of times. Straining cloths of linen and mus-lin went through such rituals of washing and boiling as had to be seen to be believed. The straining cloth and one bucket would be left on the kitchen table. Then, wearing an old beige raincoat with a white cloth spread carefully over one arm and carrying the other milk bucket, he would proceed to meet his bovine lady, looking like a rather eccentric waiter. His light tenor voice could be heard entertaining her ladyship as he kept time to the easy rhythm of his milking.

Of course if you're a fan of bull-fighting and prefer the real thing to reading Hemingway, you can see the breed of the Kerry Cow reflected in the black bulls of Spain as they take on Spanish matadors when there is sometimes death in the afternoon.

INNISFALLEN AND THE
ANNALS

It is possible that Killarney's largest lake, Loch Léin, which translates into 'The Lake of Learning', was named for the scholarship for which this one of Europe's most beautiful lakes was noted. This fame came about because of the renowned centre of learning contained within St Fionan's sixth century monastery in the island of Innisfallen. Although now a ruin, the monastery's influence extended throughout the civilised world. Here at home Brian Boru and St Brendan are said to have studied there.

But Innisfallen will always be famous because of the *Annals of Innisfallen,* a book that was written on the island and which contains a most considerable body of authentic Irish history covering three centuries – from the tenth to the thirteenth. It confirms among other facts that Ireland was fully deserving of its early title, *Ensula Sanctorum et Doctorum* – The Land of Saints and Scholars. This book from Innisfallen's golden days, which in some cases is the sole authority on events in southern Ireland over three centuries and throws light on Irish orthography and pronunciation using the old Irish script, lies in the Bodleian Library of Oxford University. It has been there since the middle of the eighteenth century, having had many different owners. Dean Swift put up a very persuasive argument to secure the *Annals* for the Library of Trinity College Dublin, but to no avail. When may we have our precious book back please? The Royal Irish Academy made a perfect facsimile in 1933 and the Dublin Institute for Advanced Studies published Seán Mac-Airt's translation in 1951. A famous extract from the *Annals* reads – the year is 1180:

> *There was committed in this year a deed which greatly vexed the clergy of all Ireland – namely the plundering of Inis Faithlen by Mael Duin, son of Donal O'Donoghue, and carrying off by him of all the worldly wealth therein, which was under the protection of its Saints, Clerics and Consecrated Churches.*

Mael Duin did indeed collect the gold, silver, trappings, mantles and cloaks of West Munster 'without any respect for God or man, but the mercy of God did not allow him to kill people or to strip this heavenly place of church furnishings or books' – the *Annals of Innisfallen* remained safe!

Near the lakeshore north-east of the monastery a lovely bijoux Hiberno-Romanesque church or abbey can be found. Dating from the twelfth century, its architectural style is thought by many to be much more in sympathy with the Irish landscape than the severe Irish Gothic style that replaced it. Many poems have been written in praise of Innisfallen, including William Allingham's long poem, 'The Abbot of Innisfallen'.

THE LAKES OF
KILLARNEY

'They say that the Lakes of Killarney are fair, no stream like the Liffey can ever compare'. So begins Dominic Behan's popular tongue-in-cheek song of the 1970s. They also say, in a reversal of the Dutch-boy-putting-his-finger-in-the-dyke-to-save-Holland story, that Loch Léin, the Lower Lake, came about because a girl forgot to replace the capstone of a well. And there, hey presto! In the ensuing flooding, Killarney's largest lake appeared. Another variation of that story tells that in the misty past the ante-diluvian town of Killarney disappeared into a deep valley west of the newly restored Ross Castle. On a clear day the shadows of old boatmen can be seen rowing their boats in the submerged streets below. Apparently, Chieftain O'Donoghue of Ross Castle wanted to get rid of an old superstitious belief that, should the strong cover not be replaced on the central well, the town would be flooded. Sure enough, a visiting jester obliged and the original town of Killarney disappeared under the waters of what is now Loch Léin.

A much more likely reason for the existence of Killarney's famous three – Loch Léin, Muckross and the Upper Lake, is glacial excavation during the last Ice Age. The lakes' foundations thus laid, the subsequent meltdown due to a warming climate, brought cascading streams from the surrounding mountains to flood the area. It was a handsome valedictory gesture from the Ice Age.

The River Laune keeps flooding to acceptable levels by taking the overflow of the Killarney Lakes into the Atlantic Ocean at Ballykissane near Killorglin, fourteen miles away. Teeming fish life and hundreds of islands abound on the lakes. The islands are uninhabited now, but for a thousand years it would seem that all human life was there. Hermits and holy people came to find their own space; scholars taught and students came to learn, while local chieftains built fortifications. In the early nineteenth century, a copper-mining industry on the tip of the Ross Peninsula is said to have yielded £80,000 profit, employing hundreds of men in the process. A barge brought the copper to Dingle Harbour from whence it was shipped to Swansea in Wales.

All kinds of adventurers came to exploit a promising situation including two Lancashire men who devised a plan to drain Loch Léin, thereby increasing the Kenmare estates. But, a couple of Killarney boatmen, ear to the ground, chased them out of it. Incidentally, it might be possible to find a boatman who will know of a still unnamed rock or island on the lakes. He might arrange to have it named after you – provided an appropriate bottle is brought along for the christening!

THE KERRY BOG PONY

Writer John B. Keane commends the Kerry Bog Pony in his most stylish prose. This equine marvel he describes as being 'elegant company … the very soul of sure-footedness and reliability'. John B. caps his eulogy with the very important insight, 'he'll eat almost anything'!

Several examples of this re-discovered beauty may be admired, talked-to, fed and ridden during a visit to the Kerry Bog Village. Situated on the Ring of Kerry between Killorglin and Glenbeigh, this attractive 'village' and its owner John Mulvihill play host to several of these endearing creatures. Indeed, it is thanks to John Mulvihill that professional interest was generated to help re-establish the identity of what transpires to be a unique breed.

Wetherbys Ireland Bloodtyping Laboratory offered its services to establish the pony's genetic basis. Taking a sample of seventy ponies, the same bloodtyping method as that carried out on thoroughbred and non-thoroughbred horses was proceeded with. The results showed the Kerry Bog Pony to be a particular breed in its own right.

Well-researched documentation by Joan Stack puts this pony, unique to Kerry, in its historical context. The first record of Kerry's Bog Ponies dates to the seventeenth-century, although there is evidence of their presence in the county long before then. Known as 'hobbies', the ponies, being strong and hardy, were ideal for drawing home the turf from the bog. They also drew seaweed to the small farmsteads along the coast. Apart from all that, they were a great source of transport.

The Kerry Bog Pony has an attractive compact appearance that is enhanced by a shaggy weatherproof coat in shades of brownish black to chestnut grey and many subtle variations in between.

Observing these gentle creatures today, it is cringe-making to think of their being used as veritable gun-fodder during the Napoleonic Wars. Only the best and strongest of them were selected for export to help supply the transport needs of the British army. They did everything from carrying soldiers to drawing heavy artillery. It is said that during the Battle of Waterloo they were formed into 'walls' and inevitably shot down or injured. Sometimes they were even eaten when food became scarce.

All of this helped to hasten their disappearance from the Kerry countryside. Also, farmers became interested in having taller horses and ponies and, by the second half of the twentieth century, mechanisation had replaced animals for transport and farm work. For the past fifty or sixty years, the Kerry Bog Pony was thought to be extinct – that is until John Mulvihill discovered one almost by accident. To him must go the credit for saving this historic breed for Kerry. Credit must also go to a few dedicated professionals who gave willingly of their time and expertise in order to re-establish the credentials of the Kerry Bog Pony.

CILL RIALAIG,
BALLINSKELLIGS

About six miles off the Ring of Kerry south-west of Cahirsiveen in the area of Ballinskelligs, a tiny isthmus, an independent little peninsula, bestrides St Finan's Bay with the confidence of a Fenian giant. A backdrop of centuries-old archaeological remains encasing this tiny neck of land suggests continuous and varied human activity from pagan times. Since the arrival of Christianity monks, scholars and nuns have long favoured it; although it was not always at peace, since one of the few Cromwellian actions in Kerry is recorded here. It is still possible to find the remains of early artistic activity: Greek and Latin crosses, inscribed stone pillars and more.

The area was ripe for a renaissance and during the 1980s when people yet again began to look for their own havens of retreat, Noelle Campbell-Sharp found herself bewitched by Cill Rialaig having gazed out over the Atlantic Ocean from Bolus Head on the south side of St Finan's Bay. The next stop across the sea is America but she knew that it was here she needed to stay.

In the Gaeltachts or Irish-speaking areas of Ireland, clusters of houses – usually stone cottages – have long been known as 'villages'. Before the nineteenth century Irish Famine, Cill Rialaig village was perched high on the cliff-top. Now, all was in ruins. Ms Campbell-Sharp decided to change all that and 'The Cill Rialaig Project' was born.

Five ruined cottages have been converted into studios. Artists, including writers, many of international repute, clamour for residencies from spring through autumn. Italian artist, Aurelio Aminatti is a frequent visitor. He says of Cill Rialaig: 'This place gives me inspiration and energy. There is nothing like this, so sincere, so wild and magical in the Mediterranean'. Many artists echo Aminatti's sentiments. Ireland is well-represented: Michael Ashur, Barry Cooke, Jane O'Malley, Barrie Castle, Liam de Freine and Elizabeth Cope are representative of many practitioners. Mick Mulcahy left a constant reminder of his three-month stay – a lively mural on the gable of the An Óige Hostel. The cottages are rent-free so each artist leaves an original work of art in appreciation.

These pictures are hung and sold in the Siopa Cill Rialaig just a couple of miles down the road in Dungeagan. Here design is again in excellent taste with the exhibition space, shopping area, restaurant and applied workshops each complementary to the other. Vibrant colour is everywhere. Home-baking aromas make a visit to the restaurant a must. Calorie counting is forgotten! Sitting round the huge turf-burning open fire you might even discover a German visitor knitting a sock, and learning how to 'turn the heel' might provide a very personal workshop!

Still wearing her badge of courage and dedication,

Ms Campbell-Sharp is already envisaging the realisation of yet another dream – the building of the most magnificent museum of modern art in Western Europe in Waterville on the Ring of Kerry.

JEANIE JOHNSTON

To enter into the mindset of passengers who sailed from Tralee on the *Jeanie Johnston* on any one of her sixteen voyages across the hazardous three thousand miles of the Atlantic Ocean to America, it is necessary to think of his or her poor physical condition from possible malnutrition and the mental stress caused by the final parting with family and friends – not to mention the apprehension engendered at the thought of facing an uncertain future on arriving into an alien culture. Reasonable fluency in the English language was probably the biggest plus of the arriving Irish émigré, as against the European nationals of the time.

Most of the Irish were as poor as church mice and physically weak, particularly inmates of workhouses – tenants of landlords who shipped them off with relief since they now had no longer a financial commitment to them under the law. North Kerry Landlord, Sir John Walsh said he had 'very great difficulty in persuading his poorer tenants to go to Quebec but considered the trouble worthwhile because of the restoration of tranquillity'. Ethnic cleansing with such condescension!

The glamour surrounding the wonderful re-incarnation which is our Millennium Mark 2 *Jeanie Johnston* cannot dim the memory of the awful Irish Famine which caused much of the history of that first pioneering *Jeanie* to be written.

The 1840's Famine was traumatic, it can still touch a raw nerve in our national consciousness. Rural Ireland was dependent on the potato for its food. A blight in the summer of 1845 destroyed the potato crop. Imported grain was substituted. In 1846, 1847 and 1848, further vicissitudes visited the potato crop. A Whig government in Britain treated the disaster with heartless disdain. More and more people died from hunger or disease. Kerry's rural population fell dramatically what with few marriages and mass emigration. And the great Kerry Champion of people, Daniel O'Connell died in 1847, having lost his last crusade – to repeal the Act of Union.

Emigration ensured that what rural Ireland lost, urban America gained. On their arrival in the New World, the young women disembarked from such ships as the *Jeanie Johnston* to enter domestic service in affluent city homes. The young men, sensibly perhaps, forsook their agricultural background and decided to stay where the women were! The young men and young women of Kerry, Cork and Limerick who sailed in the *Jeanie Johnston* on any one of her sixteen voyages from Tralee formed part of an Irish/American epic.

The general pattern of emigration at the time showed almost equal numbers of women and men. And for the men particularly this was most fortunate since, apart from a small number of Germans, Catholics were scarce on the ground and a Protestant girl would hardly look sideways at an Irish Catholic. So, their own country women provided the only chance of finding a marriage partner: Poles and Italians had not yet arrived in any great numbers.

The young Irish women and girls learned social skills while working as domestic servants in wealthy homes. But these brave emigrants learned the hard way. Largely despised by their employers, they lived in the shadows, were never addressed by their own name and so, a virtual army of 'Brigids' was formed. Yes, each girl was known in each household as 'Brigid' – and never addressed by her own name. Racism was rampant there too when the Irish refugees arrived.

A Protestant German cartoonist, Thomas Nast, made them the butt of cruel cartoons. He depicted the 'Brigids' as monkeys – no doubt for the delectation of their employers who displayed the vulgar superiority so often evidenced in the nouveau riche. But, the 'Brigids' struck back. In his book, *Banished Children of Eve, a story of New York from the Famine to the Civil War,* Peter Quinn describes how on one occasion a girl from Macroom refused to answer to 'Brigid'.

'Margaret Sir, me name is Margaret', she said to her astonished employer.

Eventually of course, Margaret and her likes took to studying in the libraries and colleges; many became secretaries, teachers and nurses and bought their own homes.

The NYPD – the New York Police Department – was for a long period synonymous with Irishness. Like people everywhere, bad apples appeared too – but that is a story for another place.

And there is many an emigrant song to remind us of the heartbreak left behind in Ireland:

> *Over the green sea, Mavourneen, Mavourneen.*
> *Long shone the white sail that bore thee away.*
> *Riding the white waves that fine summer mornin', just*
> *   like a May flower afloat on the bay.*
> *Oh but my hear sank when clouds came between us.*
> *Like a grey curtain, the rain falling down, hid from my*
> *   sad eyes the path o'er the ocean.*
> *Far, far away where my colleen had flown.*

Anonymous

ACKNOWLEDGMENTS

The author and publisher would like to thank Kathleen Browne, Kerry County Librarian and the staff at Kerry County Library, especially Michael Costelloe and staff of the local History Department for all their help.

Special thanks to all who helped to make the series possible.

Thanks are also due for permission to use copyright material: Mercier Press for material by Bob Boland and Sigerson Clifford, Micheál de Mórdha for material from his book *An Rialtas ab Fhearr! Scannán David Lean – Ryan's Daughter*, J. Anthony Gaughan for material from his book *Listowel and it's Vicinity*, Donal Horgan for material from his book *Echo After Echo*, Shannon Development, Cork Kerry Tourism, St John's Theatre and Arts Centre, The Kerry Bog Village and Noelle Campbell-Sharp for the use of their photographs.